Travel Writing
and the Empire

OUR RECENT RELEASES

Short Fiction
Katha Prize Stories 12
  Ed Geeta Dharmarajan
Best of the Nineties:
Katha Prize Stories 11
  Ed Geeta Dharmarajan
The End of Human History
  By Hasan Manzar
Hauntings: Bangla Ghost Stories
  Ed and Trans by
  Suchitra Samanta
Forsaking Paradise: Stories from
Ladakh,
  Ed and Trans by
  Ravina Aggarwal
Ayoni and Other Stories
  Ed and Trans by
  Alladi Uma & M Sridhar
Home and Away
  By Ramachandra Sharma
  Trans by Padma and
  Ramachandra Sharma

ALT (Approaches to Literatures in Translation)
Ismat: Her Life, Her Times
  Eds Sukrita Paul Kumar &
  Sadique
Translating Partition
  Eds Ravikant & Tarun K Saint
Translating Caste
  Ed Tapan Basu
Translating Desire
  Ed Brinda Bose
Vijay Tendulkar

Trailblazers
Ambai: Two Novellas and a Story
  Trans by C T Indra,
  Prema Seetharam & Uma Narayanan
Paul Zacharia: Two Novellas
  Trans by Gita Krishnankutty

Ashokamitran: Water
  Trans by Lakshmi Holmström
Bhupen Khakhar: Selected Works
  Trans by Bina Srinivasan,
  Ganesh Devy & Naushil Mehta,
Indira Goswami: Pages Stained with Blood
  Trans by Pradip Acharya

Katha Classics
Pudumaippittan
  Ed Lakshmi Holmström
Basheer Ed Vanajam Ravindran
Mauni Ed Lakshmi Holmström
Raja Rao Ed Makarand Paranjape
A Madhaviah Padmavati
  Trans Meenakshi Tyagarajan

Katha Novels
Singarevva and the Palace
  By Chandrasekhar Kambar
  Trans by Laxmi Chandrashekar
Listen Girl!
  By Krishna Sobti
  Trans by Shivanath

YuvaKatha
Lukose's Church
Night of the Third Crescent
Bhiku's Diary
The Verdict
The Dragonfly
The Bell

FORTHCOMING
Links in Our Chain
  By Mahadevi Verma
  Trans by Neera Kuckreja Sohoni
Mountain of the Moon
  By Bibhutibhushan Bandopadhyay
  Trans by Santanu Sinha Chaudhuri

Travel Writing
and the Empire

Essays by
Mohammed Zaheer Basha, Narendra Luther,
Pallavi Pandit Laisram, Pramod K Nayar,
Sindhu Menon, Susan Bassnett,
V B Tharakeshwar, Tutun Mukherjee,
William Dalrymple

Edited by
Sachidananda Mohanty

ф
KATHA

First published by Katha in 2003

Copyright © Katha, 2003

The collection as a whole © Katha, 2003
The individual contributions
© the respective authors, 2003

KATHA
A3, Sarvodaya Enclave
Sri Aurobindo Marg, New Delhi 110 017
Phone: (91-11) 4141 6600, 4141 6610
Fax: (91-11) 2651 4373
E-mail: marketing@katha.org
Website: http://www.katha.org

KATHA is a registered nonprofit organization
devoted to enhancing the joy of reading.
KATHA VILASAM is its story research and resource centre.

Series Editor: Geeta Dharmarajan
In-house Assistant Editor: Parnal Chirmuley
Production Coordinator: Sanjeev Palliwal

Book and Cover Design: Geeta Dharmarajan
Cover Painting: An English Gig (ca 1840), by Sheikh Muhammad Amir
Courtesy: Arthur M Sackler Gallery, Smithsonian Institution, Washington, D C

Typeset in 11.5 on 14.5pt Lapidary333 BT by Sandeep Kumar at Katha

ISBN 978-81-87649-36-6

First Reprint 2016

CONTENTS

ACKNOWLEDGEMENTS

Some of the papers in this volume originated in a national seminar on travel writing I coordinated under the UGC's Special Assistance Programme (SAP) of the Department of English, University of Hyderabad in March, 1999. A few other essays have been specially commissioned for this volume, which, however, does not represent the proceedings of the seminar.

I am indebted to several individuals and organizations for the making of this book:

The Chairman, Department of English, University of Hyderabad, Professor K Narayana Chandran, my faculty colleagues as well as students/scholars of the Department of English.

Professor Mohan G Ramanan, former Head and Coordinator of the UGC's Special Assistance Programme of my Department for his unreserved support.

Professor Sudhakar Marathe, former Head, Department of

. English for being particularly supportive with ideas and arrangements during the seminar.

The academic publishing unit of Katha, New Delhi, especially its Executive Director, Geeta Dharmarajan, for her keenness on this project.

Several editors of Katha through whose hands the manuscript passed: Mousumi Roy Chowdhury and Urmila Dasgupta.

To Parnal Chirmuley for her sense of professionalism, and her spirit of consideration. I also thank Gita Rajan for ably coordinating this project at Katha. Similarly, I acknowledge with thanks the editorial assistance by Shoma Choudhury.

The contributors of this volume, many of whom had initially responded to my call for papers and later submitted several revised drafts. They readily gave a great deal of their time and stood by me.

Professor Susan Bassnett and Mr William Dalrymple for allowing me the use of their essays.

Sincere gratitude to my father Sri Panchanan Mohanty for his constant push and moral support for all my academic adventures!

Finally, the real credit of this venture goes to the spirit of travel in each one of us. It is this that has clearly inspired all the contributors to this volume, as indeed the innumerable readers and critics of travel literature. This book is dedicated to them.

INTRODUCTION: BEYOND THE IMPERIAL EYE

Though travel and travel writing have always fascinated human beings ever since the dawn of human history, travel literature as a genre has been traditionally regarded as a form of entertainment and relaxation rather than as a matter worthy of serious scholarly or literary attention. True, we have always been captivated by travel narratives – Jonathan Swift's *Gulliver's Travels* and R L Stevenson's *Travels with a Donkey*, to mention only two examples. We might even confess in more honest moments that travel books of an Aldous Huxley, a D H Lawrence, or a Graham Greene might edge out other heavyweights in their sheer magic of appeal and power of captivation.

It is not just its universal appeal to human nature across all cultures that makes travel literature powerful and irresistible. In recent times, newer approaches to literary studies such as colonial discourse, gender, postcolonial, and translation studies have brought travel and travel literature to the forefront of the mainstream academia. Such approaches have contributed to a radical revision of our understanding of the literary texts and the social contexts, the politics of representation and more fundamentally, the way in which disciplines, previously seen as compartmentalized and at odds with each other, appear to mutually reinforce in terms of the gathering of knowledge and the understanding of social behaviour.

While travelling is often seen as synonymous with leisure, there are many forms of travel that are prompted by considerations other than leisure — matters of exigency and survival, for instance. Bands of hunters and food-gatherers from early human history, travelling in search of prey or fresh pastures, have been a universal phenomenon. Although it has been valorized, at times as a conscious and significant act carrying moral, intellectual and spiritual significance, it would be far from true to suggest that all travelling is exclusively or precisely of this kind. Whether at war or at peace, travel has always gone hand in hand with the march of human civilization. The image of the journey or voyage, as in *The Illiad, The Tempest, The Ramayana*, or in "The Ancient Mariner," has often served as a universal archetype for the human condition and man's turbulent passage through the world.

Indeed, if we were to think of one single term that would sum up the sustained and near-universal drive for cultural travel throughout the world ever since recorded history, it would perhaps be the *ceaseless human urge for exploration*. The drive for exploration is an insistent fact of life, constantly observed. It is repeatedly inscribed in all the great literatures of the world — the Miltonic Adam looking down on the beatific earth, Ulysses' ceaseless voyages to strive, to seek to conquer and never to yield, Prospero's magical creations in Shakespeare's island of imagination, Rasselas' yearning to leave the "Happy Valley," the epic journeys of a Dante and Virgil; or Nachiketa and Orpheus' entry into the World of the Dead. Similarly, the great Middle Eastern narratives of the Arabian Nights and Sinbad the Sailor, the travels of the spiritual pilgrim in the East, the time travellers of an H G Wells, or the scientific adventures of Jules Verne's fantasy world – all underlie the universal desire for travel.[1] It must be man's deep idealism and endless longing that make him a perpetually dissatisfied wayfarer. Indeed, following Susan Sontag we may say that all serious thought struggles with a feeling of homelessness. The traveller's deliberate denial of roots makes him a ceaseless wayfarer.

Travel writing as a genre has moved out from the earlier periphery of guide books and has come centre stage today. It has accommodated within its fold, while simultaneously critiquing the various social, cultural and ethnographic discourses that lend it a richly textured significance. It is instructive to find in this context Paul Fussell in his book *Abroad: British Literary Travelling between Wars* making a useful distinction between an explorer, traveller and tourist. As Fussell suggests:

> "Explorers," according to Hugh and Pauline Massingham, "are to the ordinary traveller what the Saint is to the average Church congregation ..." No traveller, and certainly no tourist, is ever knighted for his performances, although the strains he may undergo can be as memorable as an explorer's. All three make journeys, but the explorer seeks the undiscovered, the traveller, that which has been discovered by the mind working in history, the tourist that which has been discovered by entrepreneurship and prepared for him by the arts of mass publicity. The genuine traveller is, or used to be, in the middle between the two extremes. If the explorer moves towards the risks of the formless and the unknown, the tourist moves towards the security of pure cliché. It is between these two poles that the traveller mediates, retaining all he can of the excitement or the unpredictable attaching to exploration and fusing that with the pleasure of "knowing where one is" belonging to tourism.[2]

While much of postcolonial theory today tends to equate travel invariably with empire, recent works such as the one by Joan Pao Rubies entitled *Travel and Ethnicity in the Renaissance,* suggests that there is actually a sense of diversity in the European perception of the rest of the world from fourteenth to the nineteenth century, "that travellers may reproduce local knowledge and prejudices as much as import some of their own ..."[3] What Rubies allows us to see is the pre history of an imperial discourse without allowing us the lazy comfort of a teleology which sees Renaissance travel accounts as a prelude to the Orientalists' imagination.[4]

It is, however, noteworthy that the advent of large empires, beginning with the early nineteenth century in different parts of the world, gave rise to special forms of travel. Of course, it would be erroneous and plainly unhistorical to suggest that colonial travel did not exist prior to the nineteenth century. In Europe itself, the exploits of conquerors such as Alexander the Great, Hannibal and Napoleon inspired travel for conquest and subjugation. Not all individuals were motivated by the spirit of exploitation and appropriation, however. Several had more honourable intentions, and undertook journeys braving formidable obstacles for the sake of building cultural bridges as Huen Tsang did in seventh Century AD. It is true that the question of motive is analyzed critically within the academia today. However, we may be making a serious error by ignoring the issue or treating it as completely suspect.

However, it testifies to the power of the colonial state and not so subtle systems of rewards and punishments that the colonial administrative apparatus was capable of promoting cultural travel of a select kind. The collusion and coalition between the colonial state and cultural institutions such as are manifest in the School of Oriental and African Studies (SOAS) begun by George V, reveals points of contact between knowledge and power. It is instructive to note that institutions like the SOAS that are recognized today for carrying out valuable research had earlier enjoyed a colonial mandate.

It is only now that we are beginning to understand the full extent of this interface and its debilitating influence. The "willing consent" of the ruled based on the internalization of colonial values at the deeper psychological level offers us instructive lessons for understanding colonial travel, then as well as now. Narratives of the nineteenth century, both adventure as well as science fiction, repeatedly enact their stories on a soil that presents itself as remote and exotic. H Rider Haggard's adventure novels or Edgar Rice Burroughs' celebrated Tarzan tales set in the deepest forests of Africa, recurrently punctuate the narrative with the mines of a King Solomon or civilizations of the Lost Whites in the heart of black Africa, just as Starship *Enterprise's* journey into outer space may represent the ultimate in Western imagination for conquest and colonization.

Indeed, Mary Louise Pratt in her pioneering work *Imperial Eyes: Travel Writing and Transculturation,* formulates the important concept of "contact zones." These zones, according to her, are "social spaces where disparate cultures meet, clash and grapple with each other, often in highly asymmetrical relations of domination and subordination."[5] Thus, travel writing is viewed as one of the ideological apparatuses of the empire. Pratt uses the term "transculturation" to describe how subordinate groups absorb dominant cultures. Contact zones, according to her, are determined by the extent of transculturation.

Thus, sponsored or institution-backed travel in the late eighteenth and nineteenth centuries, even when carried out under the guise of a more honorific study and research, often concealed a set of aims, objectives and agenda ulterior in motive. The rapid growth of area studies in Western universities often went hand in hand with the colonial enterprise. The introduction of foreign language schools for the study of regional cultures was prompted, for the most part, by the need to generate a favourable climate for conducting diplomacy, commerce, business, and also war.[6] The institutional history of many such centres in Britain, France and Belgium, the major colonial powers, often parallels the trajectory of their overseas missions and their cultural empire in the postcolonial period – French-speaking enclaves in North and West Africa, Anglophone nations in Asia and Africa, and Spanish-speaking Latin America. Knowledge of the history of colonial institutions adds immeasurably to our understanding of power and patronage behind cultural travel. While culture is ostensibly treated as a soft option, the mobilization of colonial resources, both by the State as well as through private efforts, indicates the historic role actually played by sponsored travel in the domestication of the colonial empire.[7]

II

While it would be sweeping to push all travel literature under an all-purpose political or imperial design, the fact remains that it is during the consolidation of large empires in the nineteenth century that we see travel literature betraying a particular awareness of the ideological and political. That is how travel writing often became a site for the collision and contestation of power. Such accounts could be variously read as a means of cultural domination and appropriation, and alternately as identity formation under colonial rule.

Indeed, it is only now that we are beginning to realize in India, thanks to the new scholarship in the field of gender, tribal, minorities, ethnic and subaltern studies, the disturbingly pronounced use of the travel motif for cultural appropriation. The exhibition of our tribal population, their lifestyle and heritage through safari-like travel, results inevitably in cultural tourism, just as the display, sale and consumption of ethnic ware, through the pan-Indian cinema and advertisement campaigns, result in the commodification of culture.

The passage of our exotic North East through the Republic Day tableaux may bolster the Indian State and its increasing reliance on the military, but it conceals the many wars of attrition and insurrection, pervasive in our near-breakaway provinces.

We see a similar pattern in the use of the travel motif of the colonial kind in the world of advertisement. The sex appeal evoked by the exhilarating puff of a Charms cigarette or the welcome sip of Nescafe always precedes in cinemascope a controlled adventure in the cinematic jungle. The hero's destined encounter with a domestic man-eater forever wins gratitude from the maiden in distress around the glowing campfire, just as the advertisement for Bajaj Sunny, the popular two-wheeler, shows the White traveller merrily riding off into the distance as the group of blacks gape helpless, stupified.

Several categories are often seen embodied in travel motifs that are deployed in the advertisement world and elsewhere: orality-literacy, nature-nurture, primitivism-civilization. Similarly, the celebration of the exotic through such recurrent images as vacation cruises to Tangiers and Casablanca or voyages to Congo, Sierra Leone or India reveal the working of the "Orientalist" and other fantasies. These could range from the enormously popular tales like *The Sheikh* set in the Middle East and other texts mentioned by Ketaki Dyson in a *A Various Universe*,[8] to those by sophisticated travel writers such as D H Lawrence, Graham Greene, Aldous Huxley, Mark Twain, Harriet Tytler, Carlos Fuentes, Pico Iyer, as well as British and American travellers in India.

With the advent of colonial modernity in the nineteenth century in India, we see a form of colonial travel within India as a geographical space. The element of keenness and curiosity evidenced by those who took the early Indian railways, for instance, can be seen in early travelogues in the various Indian languages. In the Oriya author Sashibhushan Ray's *Dakhinatya Bhramana*, (Travel to the South), 1897, for example, we see precisely such a trend. There is much of local colour here, aside from a discovery of new lands and regions. But there is also the self's encounter with the mighty power of the British Empire. Similar narratives, many of which have been discovered by archival research, would clearly enhance a better understanding of travel and colonial rule in British India.

Twentieth century travel writing by Western authors displays richly complex and often rewarding ways of dealing with the exotic. Michael Wood's *The Smile of Murugan* or William Dalrymple's *Delhi: The City of Djinns* are interesting examples of this trend. Components of John Master's fictional narratives are open to an Orientalist reading. Similarly, diasporic Indian academics and physicians like Abraham Verghese offer travel narratives that serve as a typical *rite de passage* to a new world. On the other hand, according to some, even "progressive" travel writers are not free from the colonial gaze. For instance, Ilija Trojanow contends that "progressive" intellectuals like Günter Grass and Pier Paolo Pasolini, champions of the Left, "mirror the imperial hegemony of the first world while simultaneously denouncing it. By refusing to enter into a relationship with what they describe, by refusing to lose themselves in the unknown and let themselves be changed, they deny differences and the evolution of a hybrid discourse."[9]

Travel in the twentieth century thus comes through an amazing variety of ways such as diaspora, migration, exile, excursion and exploration and there is rich literature in each of these categories. One of the significant manifestations of travel in this sense is travel account by women. Following the theoretical formulations of Mary Louise Pratt and Sara Mills, women critics like Margaret Macmillan, Indira Ghose, and Indrani Sen have critically studied the women travel writers of the Raj. They argue that colonial space was a gendered terrain. They explore the interface between colonialism and gender representation. This is a new and fruitful area of enquiry that opens up newer avenues of research into travel writing from the woman's point of view.

Another interesting dimension of travel in the twentieth century has been with regard to the issue of faith or pilgrimage. We see in this context travel accounts of writers like Paul Brunton and Sister Nivedita. To what extent their sympathetic narratives of India were free from the colonial bias is a matter for debate and exploration.

That travel writing is more than a geographical account, local colour, spirit of place, or depiction of manners and morals, and is actually a form of a memoir, an autobiography, dates back to Emerson and Thoreau, if not to the earlier masters. What is radically new is perhaps the perception that travel books map out the territories of the mind, define contours of nations and communities, and determine forms of cultural and political representations. They mediate across disciplinary boundaries and knowledge systems. Thus, while the earlier approaches retain their charm and validity, the newer ones pose challenges to our earlier paradigms. Properly handled, they illuminate our understanding of society and culture.

III

This volume is based on the assumption that travel writing's intersection with the empire, especially during the nineteenth century, ends in a unique configuration. Travel narratives especially in the postcolonial context often become self-assuring exercises, a site for the collision and contestation of cultures, and for the natives the internalization of their subject status. India has been a particular site for this kind of writing. Recent developments in theory have also made travel writing a more fruitful area in cultural study. Viewed from this angle, many travel books seem to show an enigmatic mix of conflicting drives. William Dalrymple's well known novel *The White Mughals* provides an interesting example of such a cultural mix.

The main focus of this study is the Indo-British cultural encounter through the mode of travel, although there is a comparative perspective from Persia as well.

The volume attempts to bring together a set of reflective essays that straddle many disciplines and newly emerging areas of study such as colonial discourse, gender, and postcolonial studies. It contains ten chapters, all of which are focussed on the imperial dimension of travel writing. While the introduction believes that travel is not always foredoomed to a colonial gaze and can aspire to look beyond the imperial eye, the contributors to the volume negotiate and answer this question in varied ways.

"Travel Writing and British Studies" by Susan Bassnett, explains the primary reasons as to why travel writing has come centre stage today. This essay, it may be said, offers a rationale for the preparation of this volume. As the opening chapter, it unveils exciting possibilities latent in the emerging discipline of travel writing as a genre.

In the next chapter, "Hajji Baba: Ideological Basis of the Persian Picaro," Pallavi Pandit Laisram examines nineteenth century European construction of Persia through a specific novel with a travel motif. There is a rich understanding here of the Islamic world vis à vis the Western perceptions of the Middle East. Following Susan Bassnett's excellent introduction to the theme of travel, as a corollary, this essay offers an important comparative perspective regarding the colonial gaze of the Orient as manifest in Western travel accounts of Persia.

Continuing the theme of Western travel accounts, albeit of a radically different kind, "Porous Boundaries and Cultural Crossover: Fanny Parkes and 'Going Native'" by the British travel writer William Dalrymple, underlines hybridities and mixed motives that characterize some of the Indo-British encounters. Dalrymple argues that the earlier interactions between the British and the native Indians, as recorded in travel accounts by Fanny Parkes, prior to 1857, suggest a greater mingling in inter racial terms. This account is in refreshing contrast to some of the recent postcolonial thinking that suggests a more rigid boundary line between the colonial rulers and the natives.

An important dimension of the colonial rule in India was the British Prison system or remote islands such as the Andamans, known as Kala pani that acted as penitentiaries. "Colonialism, Surveillance and Memoirs of Travel: Tegart's Diaries and the Andaman Cellular Jail" by Tutun Mukherjee relates memoirs of British functionaries with colonial incarcerations. It specifically looks at a very interesting dimension of the machinery of the colonial state. Thereby, the chapter promotes the discourse on colonial travel in India.

In continuation of the same theme with a different subject matter, "Propaganda as Travelogue: A Study of Katherine Mayo's *Mother India*" by Mohammed Zaheer Basha, makes a fresh assessment of *Mother India*, earlier castigated by M K Gandhi. This book, we may recall, became a powerful instrument for the national freedom struggle. It is a critique of Mayo that continues the traditional reading of the text.

The following chapter, "Constitutive Contradiction: Travel Writing and Construction of Native Women in Colonial India" by Sindhu Menon reveals a new dimension to the colonial travel. It offers an admirable interface between travel literature and gender studies. It suggests that Western "male travellers often give lyrical accounts of the appearance and appeal of the Indian women."

Taking the discussion to a hitherto unexplored area, Pramod K Nayar's "Touring Aesthetics: The Colonial Rhetoric of Travel Brochures Today," shows the texts of travel brochures in India containing colonial rhetoric. It adopts a "literary approach" locating certain tropological features in them. It concludes that the tourist brochures create "both a *shikari* (hunter) and an aesthete in its tourist." This chapter deals with an important aspect of the popular sub-culture in India from the point of view of colonial travel.

In recent years, new and fruitful research has been carried out in the field of regional literature and culture in India. In "Empire Writes Back? Kannada Travel Fiction and Nationalist Discourse" by V B Tharakeshwar, we see a fresh dimension that links travel writing with nationalist discourse, especially in Karnataka. It attempts to explore "the process of the formation of a nationalist identity through travels as witnessed in the Kannada travelogues and also in Kannada fiction where travel is major component." This is an area that is currently under debate in many social scientific disciplines.

A fascinating but little known aspect of colonial travel has been recorded by those who visited the courts of kings and nawabs during the eighteenth and nineteenth centuries. "Hyderabad Through Foreign Eyes" by Narendra Luther, is an emblematic account of the seat of the Deccan as seen through the eyes of foreigners.

The essays, logically connected, thus deal with the interface between the travel narrative and the empire. They speak in many voices and assume many positionalities. That the empire is alive and well despite political emancipation of the former colonies, is an unstated assumption of postcolonial thinking. And yet, it seems to me that travel narratives *can* overcome the Manichean divide between cultures and establish bondings across political frontiers.

Notes

1   For an excellent record of cultural travel from ancient times to AD 1600, see J G Links, *Travellers in Europe: Private Records of the Great and the Forgotten*, (London: Bodleyhead,1990).

2   Paul Fussell, *Abroad: British Literary Travelling between the Wars*, (New York: Oxford University Press, 1980).

3   Joan Pao Rubies, *Travel and Ethnology in the Renaissance*, (Cambridge: Cambridge University Press, 2000).

4   Dilip Menon, "Traveller as Historian" *The Hindu, Sunday Literary Review*, 2nd September, 2001.

5   Mary Louise Pratt, *Imperial Eyes: Travel Writing and Transculturation*, (London: Routledge, 1992).

6   As is well known, Edward Said's *Orientalism* (1978), provides an early account of the collusion between cultural travel and colonialism, especially in the Near East. Similarly, European male erotica of vacation cruises in Tangiers, Casablanca or Cairo betrays insistent undertones of the exotic and the unbridled (at times forbidden) sexuality. Another mode of appropriation.

7   For a related treatment of the same issue, please see my book, *In Search of Wonder: Understanding Cultural Exchange*, (New Delhi: Vision Books, 1997).

8   Ketaki Dyson, *A Various Universe: The Journals and Memories of British Men and Women in the Indian Subcontinent, 1765-1856*, (Delhi: Oxford University Press, 1978).

9   Ilija Trojanow, "Imperial Politics in the Progressive Gaze," *The Hindu*, Literary Supplement, 2nd December, 2001.

References

1   Fussell, Paul, *Abroad: British Literary Travelling between the Wars*, (New York: Oxford University Press), 1980.

2   Ghose, Indira, ed, *Memsahibs Abroad: Writings by Women Travellers in Nineteenth Century India*, (Delhi: Oxford University Press, 1988).

3   Dyson, Ketaki, *A Various Universe: The Journals and Memories of British Men and Women in the Indian Subcontinent, 1765-1856*, (Delhi: Oxford University Press, 1978).

4   Menon, Dilip, "Traveller as Historian," *The Hindu*, Sunday Literary Review, 2nd Septemeber, 2001.

5   Mills, Sara, *Discourses of Difference: An Analysis of Women's Travel Writing and Colonialism*, (London: Routledge, 1993).

6   Mohanty, Sachidananda, *In Search of Wonder: Understanding Cultural Exchange*, (New Delhi: Vision Books, 1997).

7   Pratt, Mary Louise, *Imperial Eyes: Travel Writing and Transculturation*, (London: Routledge, 1992).

8   Rubies, Joan Pao, *Travel and Ethnology in the Renaissance*, (Cambridge: Cambridge University Press, 2000).

9   Sontag, Susan, "The Anthropologist as Hero," in *Against Interpretation and other Essays*, (New York: Dell, 1978).

10 Trojanow, Ilija, "Imperial Politics in the Progressive Gaze," *The Hindu*, Literary Supplement, 2nd December, 2001.

THE EMPIRE, TRAVEL WRITING, AND BRITISH STUDIES

SUSAN BASSNETT

There is great interest in travel writing at the present time. Bookshops have whole sections devoted to the genre; new journals have emerged in the 1990s, and the names of diverse generations of travel writers such as Geoffrey Moorhouse, Eric Newby, Colin Thubron or Dervla Murphy, and even younger writers such as Bill Bryson, Nick Danziger or William Dalrymple are regularly seen in British bestseller lists. Clearly, there is a demand for their kind of writing, though it is important to note that the demand is relatively localized; the great interest in travel writing is predominantly a British phenomenon, not even an English language phenomenon. The very category of travel writing is not universal, and there are many literary systems that do not distinguish travel writing as a distinctive form at all.

However, there is currently great interest in studying travel writing, and this interest is not so localized. One of the key figures in this field, the Canadian Mary Louise Pratt, points out in the Preface to her seminal book, *Imperial Eyes*, that she taught a course on travel writing and European expansion at Stanford as long ago as 1978. As the title of Pratt's book suggests, there is a direct link between travel writing and the history of imperialism and colonization. Hence the interest in this postcolonial moment in examining the implications of texts produced by travellers from the initial period of European voyages of discovery.

The purpose of this essay, however, is to consider aspects of travel writing within the expanding field of British Studies. Key issues significant to both these interdisciplines include the problematics of defining travel writing as a genre, of tracing its origins, of considering who writes it and why, who reads it and why it should emerge as a popular form at certain significant moments in time. Perhaps, more fundamentally, it is important to ask, within the context of British Studies, what travel writing can tell us about how one culture constructs its image of other cultures.

Literary Travel

Pratt argues that travel writing is intrinsically linked to the processes of colonization. Still, it is important not to lose sight of the fact that travel writing has a long history, as does the use of travel as a literary device. The metaphor of the journey that represents the passage through life is firmly established in the literatures of many cultures around the world. Dante Alighieri's great journey through Hell, Purgatory and Paradise in his *The Divine Comedy* begins with the famous image of being lost in a dark wood midway through his life. This is a familiar image in Jungian psychology – the traveller, i.e., Everyman, who loses his way at a certain point in his existence and has to be shown the true path to enlightenment. It cannot be accidental that the great cycles of European medieval poetry all concern travel – the journeying of Orlando and his fellow knights, the quests of King Arthur and the denizens of Camelot, the great seafaring journeys of the Norse sagamen.

The popularity of this trope reflects the processes of movement and change in feudal, pre-urban societies. It is significant that once the processes of urbanization began, the quest theme lost much of its appeal. It is also interesting that at the point when European society was changing into a more recognizable shape for us today, in what we may loosely term the Early Modern period, a great deal of energy and interest was going into expansion outside the boundaries of Europe. The great cycles of heroic questing were accompanied, in the later stages, by the journeys of Henry the Navigator, and by an unprecedented fascination for map-making, and for improving the scientific devices required to undertake long-distance travel. By the sixteenth century, the wandering knight, on his eternal quest through the forests, was replaced in popular imagination by the seafarer, bringing back strange treasures from unknown lands beyond the horizon.

Struggling to find a language with which to describe what they saw, travellers often borrowed from the romances they were familiar with. Hence the extraordinary accounts that came back with the ship – accounts of amazing creatures with several heads, superhuman strength, astonishing colours, and unbelievable eating habits. Gabriel Garcia Marquez, in his Nobel Prize address in 1982, pointed out how the fantastical depictions of the Americas by European travellers created an idea of a continent full of marvels and bizarre realities, a perception that continues to the present day, and which, he argues, is all too often detrimental.

Describing and categorizing things that were seen for the first time was, in the early years of the voyages, unscientific as they were inspired by the romances that were the equivalents of popular fiction. The letters of Columbus, for example, are full of references to being on the brink of discovering the extraterrestrial lands. In the account of his third voyage in 1498, he writes: "There are powerful signs of the presence of the earthly Paradise, for the place accords with the opinions of those holy and sacred theologians"[1]

Alongside what might be termed the fantastical realism of travellers' tales, there is another powerful literary tradition – the use of the travel account for satirical purposes. In this tradition, a fictitious traveller is created who comments on the places he visits from a naïve perspective. Goldsmith's Chinese traveller to England in *Citizen of the World*, or Swift's Gulliver, in different ways criticize their own English society. Likewise, Defoe's Moll Flanders can be seen as a character whose experiences give the author an opportunity to make critical comments on his own society.

The use that satirists have made of the travellers' tale reminds us of Plato, who was not in favour of travel at all because he felt that it could be a threat to his own culture. Only trustworthy elderly men, according to Plato, should be allowed to travel, and even then, their accounts should be carefully scrutinized by the authorities. The contrast that travel accounts can offer between what are the norms at home and alternative norms can be potentially very subversive indeed.

Travel as Tourism and Diplomacy

In the latter part of the eighteenth century, the emergent middle classes began to engage in the newly popular pursuit that has since become part of common life experience in the West – tourism. The phenomenon of the Grand Tour, with which we are all so familiar, when young men (and later women too) were sent on an educational tour of Europe, became increasingly popular. Roger Hudson, in his entertaining book *The Grand Tour, 1592-1796*, points out that the dreadful state of English universities was a significant factor in the initial phase of popularizing foreign travel since fathers preferred to spend their money sending their sons abroad. One example of the dreadful state of British universities may be found in 1733, when Christ's College Cambridge admitted only three students.

Edward Gibbon defined the ideal traveller of 1763 as follows:

> He should be endowed with an active, indefatigable vigour of mind and body, which can seize every mode of conveyance and support with a careless smile every hardship of the road, the weather or the inn. I must stimulate him with a restless curiosity, impatient of ease, covetous of time and fearless of danger ... with a copious stock of classical and historical learning, my traveller must blend the practical knowledge of husbandry and manufactures; he should be a chemist, a botanist, and a master of mechanics. A musical ear will multiply the pleasures of his Italian tour; but a correct and exquisite eye, which commands the landscape of a country, discerns the merits of a picture and measures the proportions of a building is more closely connected with the finer feelings of the mind ...[2]

Such exaggeratedly high-blown expectations were predictably satirized by eighteenth century writers who saw reality rather differently. Alexander Pope, in *The Dunciad*, drew a portrait of the young English traveller as a stupid, drunken, self-indulgent wastrel learning nothing except the latest hit-song, a vision that would not be out of place today when recalling some of the English tourists on the Costa Brava.

Tourism, of course, was not confined to Europe, and soon extended eastward. It was at this point, with the burgeoning industry of guidebook production, dictionaries and phrase books for the tourist trade, that the literary traditions of travel accounts converged with another, completely separate tradition – the travel accounts produced for official purposes, the letters and reports from government officials, ambassadors, trade delegates, military figures.

Familiar early texts include the accounts of Suetonius, Roman commander in Britain in 61 AD, who later became the first Roman to cross the Atlas Mountains; Othere and Wulfstan, reporting back to King Alfred; Marco Polo; Friar Odoric, who travelled through Asia for fourteen years in the early fourteenth century; Ambassador Clavijo, the Spanish envoy to the court of Tamberlaine the Great. These accounts were written for a specific purpose, that of transmitting useful information to the home culture, and they contain a great deal of detail. Here, for example, is an extract from the account of a journey to the court of Kuyuk Khan undertaken in 1245-47 by Friar John of Pian de Carpini:

> The Mongols, or Tartars, in outward shape, are unlike to all other people. For they are broader between the eyes and the balls of their cheeks, than men of other nations. They have flat and small noses, little eyes and eyelids standing straight upright, they are shaven on the crowns like priests. They wear their hair somewhat longer about the ears than upon their foreheads; but behind they let it grow long like women's hair, which they braid into two locks, binding each of them behind either ear. They have short feet also.[3]

His account is full of this kind of minute anthropological detail, carefully noting the customs, appearance, eating habits and social rituals of the people he encountered. It is obvious that this kind of text is target-focussed. There is a clear purpose in producing such an account. In the first place, it is being written for someone specific, and so a perspective on the lands and people visited by the writer is synthesized into an accessible form. The writer acts as a kind of translator, reading the signs he encounters on his journey and endeavouring to translate them for his target reader. Indeed, it is helpful to think of travel writing as closely linked to translation, for a similar relationship obtains in that there are two distinct poles – the culture of the writer and the culture that is depicted, and only the writer has access to both. The reader has to take on trust the version presented, because only the traveller has first-hand experience of what is being described, just as the translator alone has first-hand knowledge of the source knowledge. Moreover, like a translator, the travel writer is creating a text for consumption by readers at home, and in consequence, a study of the kind of writing that becomes popular at different moments in time can tell us a great deal about that particular culture. For instance, we can learn a lot about Britain by reading accounts of foreigners produced by British travellers.

The Veracity of Travel Accounts

From this briefest of sketches of the diachronics of European travel writing, it is apparent that there are all kinds of literary conventions involving travel, both literal and metaphorical. There is also a strong element of fantasy, and a whole line of travel writing that is premised on the fantastical – from Coleridge's Ancient Mariner to Star Trek or the intergalactic journeyings of the protagonists of novels by Ursula Le Guin or Doris Lessing.

Travel accounts as literature are enormously varied, and offer a rich field of study. On the other hand, there is travel writing that purports to offer first-hand truthful accounts of other cultures, and is premised on a principle of veracity. The texts mentioned so far in this category are those that were specially commissioned for specific purposes. But as has also been suggested, particularly in respect of the accounts of early travellers to the Americas, the line between the fictitious and the factual is difficult to define. In other words, travel writing faces the reader head on with the problem of boundaries.

This may, in part, explain something of the fascination that travel writing as a distinct genre is currently exercising in Britain, a society characterized by enormous changes that involve redefining all kinds of boundaries, from devolution on the political level to redefining parameters of spirituality. British society is becoming increasingly multi-ethnic, thereby creating a new space in which to model appropriate new rituals. The old boundaries have no validity in a changed social environment, and out of this sense of uncertainty comes an interest in books that provide accounts of other cultures, books that focus upon difference.

It cannot be accidental that the previous great age of travel writing was the nineteenth century, the period when Britain was the greatest power in the world, both economically and politically, seeing itself as the hub of a great empire that stretched around the world. In this present moment, when Britain is undergoing radical transformations, of which the most emblematic is Scottish and Welsh devolution, there is a vogue for a certain kind of travel writing that is unprecedented in this century. What can be deduced from this is that in times of great change, people look comparatively at their own culture, seeking to explore alternative models, and at the same time, taking an interest in books that offer alternative perspectives on the familiar. Such a model is familiar to us from Translation Studies, where Polysystems theorists have shown that translation activity is at its highest when cultures are undergoing radical periods of social and political change.

Mary Louise Pratt uses the term "contact zone" to refer to what she calls the space of colonial encounters, "in which people geographically and historically separated come into contact with each other and establish ongoing relations."[4] However, she sees this contact zone not as a neutral space but as a space charged with conflict, both actual and potential. For, as Edward Said points out in his *Orientalism*, there is an intrinsic power relationship in the writing of accounts of other cultures. Said's focus is on those writers who write about the Orient, but his assumptions can be applied to travel writing more generally. The Orientalist, says Said, "writes about something," in contrast to the Oriental who is written about. The one becomes the object of the other's study, and in consequence is placed in a passive role. Said views this difference as disturbing because it implies an inequality in the relationship between observer and observed:

> The Oriental is given as fixed, stable, in need of investigation, in need even of knowledge about himself. No dialectic is either desired or allowed. There is a source of information (the Oriental) and a source of knowledge (the Orientalist). In short, a writer and a subject matter otherwise inert.[5]

Orientals and their culture are, therefore, packaged for consumption by Western readers. Moreover, the underlying assumption is that the presentation of the Oriental (or perhaps we should simply say, the Other) is that of negative comparison between the civilized traveller (and by implication, the civilized readers for whom he/she is writing) and the uncivilized inhabitants of the home culture.

This contrast between civilized and uncivilized, which obviously leads to an unequal relationship in the depiction of the Other, is premised upon the idea of the fixity of the subject. The starting point for an account of something that has been observed is, as David Spurr (1993) points out, looking. Visual observation is the key and the point of departure simultaneously. But visual observation is subjective. And here we come to the nub of the problem, for travel writing is a discourse that is premised upon objective representation of another reality, even though that representation cannot be subjective. In an essay on two travel writers of the seventeenth and eighteenth centuries, Stephen Bann discusses the

9

view of Louis Marin that the ideology of travel implies a departure from one place and a return to the same place enriched with "the booty of knowledge." How can the traveller return to the same place, Bann asks, since not only is there a time lapse (and although not all travellers are away for more than a dozen years, all are away for some time), but the very experience of travelling will also change the individual. The traveller, then, experiences things that change his/her life and alter his/her relationship with his/her own culture.

Questions of Identity

Travel also involves issues of identity. Sometimes, it even involves transformations of identity, as some of the extraordinary examples of many women travellers of the nineteenth century and early twentieth century appear to confirm. Isabella Bird, who journeyed through some of the most hostile regions of the world and recounts hardships that appear barely imaginable, was a semi-invalid who began her travels as a result of medical advice. Having cared for aged parents until the age of forty, she was diagnosed as suffering from a debilitating spinal complaint, acute insomnia, and depression. These physical difficulties did not stop her from travelling to Hawaii, Japan, China, Tibet, Kurdistan and the Rocky Mountains, where she appeared to enjoy not only good health but extreme fitness and resilience.[6]

Similarly, Mary Kingsley led a life of dull domesticity at home nursing her invalid mother and sickly younger brother. Then suddenly, she found herself alone after her parents' death, and at the age of thirty went off to West Africa, trekking through uncharted jungles in her corsets, and consequently wrote two best-selling books on her scientific expeditions.

These two cases involve dramatic shifts of identity for, in each case, the woman at home appears barely recognizable as the woman abroad. It is hardly surprising that there is a growing body of research into women travellers, for the gap between their achievements overseas and their expectations and lives at home is enormous. Travel, in many cases, appears to have provided the space necessary for them to assert themselves, a space denied to them within the conventions of their upbringing in British society.

It also seems to have enabled some women to realize their own sexuality in ways that would have been unthinkable at home. Margaret Fountaine (1862-1940), for example, travelled the world for twenty-five years with her Syrian lover, Khalil Neimy, each equipped with a bicycle and a butterfly net. Her diaries have only recently been edited and published, but the combination of scientific rigour and open expression of desire is extraordinary, a far cry from the image of the Angel in the House, the model for Victorian womanhood.

Writing the Self

Travel writing also comes close to autobiography. William Kinglake, author of one of the classic nineteenth century travel texts, *Eothen*, is quite explicit about how the text is a product of the writer's subjectivity. For Kinglake, the task is to balance one's personal impressions and feelings with the responsibility of the writer to give what he calls some "true ideas" of the country through which one passes. He defines his traveller in the following terms:

> His very selfishness – his habit of referring the whole external world to his own sensations, compels him, as it were, in his writings, to observe the laws of perspective; he tells you of objects, not as he knows them to be, but as they seemed to him. The people, and the things that most concern him personally, however mean and insignificant, take large proportions in his picture because they stand so near to him. He shows you his Dragoman, and the gaunt features of his Arabs, his tent, his kneeling camels, his baggage strewn upon the sand; but the proper wonders of the land – the cities, the

mighty ruins and monuments of bygone ages, he throws back faintly into the distance ... You may listen to him forever without learning much in the way of Statistics; but perhaps if you bear with him long enough, you may find yourself slowly and faintly impressed with the realities of Eastern Travel.[7]

Kinglake is talking about himself here, of course, and if we start to compare different travel writers, what is apparent straight away is not the homogeneity of the genre but the enormous difference between writers. These differences have not yet been adequately analyzed, and this is another rich area for future research. Obviously there are stylistic differences, differences of tone, different emphases, et cetera, and there are also differences conditioned by the initial targeting of the work. For, even as we talk about "travel writing," we are on very slippery ground. What makes Kinglake's book significant is that it is an early example of non-scientific travel writing, and it was a bestseller. As Jan Morris points out in her introduction to the 1982 reprint:

Its effect upon the art of travel writing has been profound, and its influences may be traced down the generations from Robert Curzon's *Monasteries of the Levant* (1849) to Robert Byron's *Road to Oxiana* (1937) or Paul Theroux's *Great Railway Bazaar* (1975).[8]

The Kinglake of the end of the twentieth century may well be Bill Bryson. His books are hugely successful, and his *Notes From a Small Island* stayed on the bestseller lists in Britain for over two years. The opening paragraph of this highly personal comic account of an American's perception of England, from the 1970s to the 1990s, sets the tone for the rest of the book:

My first sight of England was on a foggy March night in 1973 when I arrived on the midnight ferry from Calais. For twenty minutes, the terminal area was aswarm with activity as cars and lorries poured forth, customs people did their duties and everyone made for the London road. Then abruptly all was silence and I wandered through sleeping, low-lit streets threaded with fog, just like in a Bulldog Drummond movie. It was rather wonderful having an English town all to myself.

The only mildly dismaying thing was that all the hotels and guesthouses appeared to be shut up for the night.[9]

Bryson's technique is to use very simple sentence structures, constantly demolishing any hints of literariness. The lyricism of the fictitious image of foggy England is immediately undercut by the realization that he isn't going to find anywhere to sleep. He depicts himself as a sentimental traveller of the modern age, rather slow on the uptake, and as an idealist who strives to hold onto his illusions regardless. Poking fun at the strangeness of English institutions and practices, appalling food and amateurishness, he nevertheless concludes his journey with a hymn of praise for the country he chose to settle down in:

What other country, after all, could possibly have come up with names like Tooting Bed and Farleigh Wallop, or a game like cricket that goes on for three days and never seems to start? Who else would think it not the least bit odd to make judges wear little mops on their heads, compel the Speaker of the House of Commons to sit on something called the Woolsack, or take pride in a military hero whose dying wish was to be kissed by a fellow named Hardy?[10]

Bryson writes not so much *about* the English as *for* the English. His book is not an attempt to provide armchair travellers with accounts of distant places that they might aspire to visit, but rather to bolster their confidence in what they have close at hand. Hence the interesting move back across the Atlantic. Bryson is an outsider who has double vision; having lived in England for so many years, he can shift between the perspective of foreigner and native. This is the quality that makes his work so appealing to large numbers of readers. It could be argued that he writes from a position of immense flexibility, and that at this point in time, in Britain, flexibility is perceived as a virtue. He plays with stereotypes of Englishness, but ultimately deconstructs them.

Fantasies of Empire

Bill Bryson is one of many bestselling travel writers in Britain today, though significantly, he writes about familiar landscapes and societies. Other writers choose less well known regions, and one in particular stands out as exerting a particular fascination for British readers of the 1990s – Central Asia. Writers of several generations, from Geoffrey Moorhouse, Colin Thubron and Peter Hopkirk to Nick Danziger and Giles Whittell have written highly successful books about this part of the world. Central Asia appears to be the locus of fantasy for many travellers, and the fantasy is directly linked to its nineteenth century imperial history. It is an area without clearly defined borders or frontiers, other than those created by geography, an area that has constantly been overrun by invading hordes, both from the West (the Greeks reached what is now Afghanistan) and from the East. It is an area where religions, languages, ethnic groups of various kinds have met, clashed, mingled or moved on. It represents the outer limits of the West, and from the opposite perspective, the outer limits of the East. The inhospitable climate and geography mean that traditionally, populations have been either nomadic or very isolated, with communication routes absolutely fundamental to their existence, but difficult to traverse. It is the territory through which the Silk Road passed, and in the nineteenth century – when the British established themselves firmly in India and the Russians began to seek access to all-year ports – it was the territory across which the Great Game was played out. And, at the end of the twentieth century, there was a revival of interest in the territories of the Great Game (Dalrymple 1990; Glazebrook 1992; Hopkirk 1993; Hopkirk 1990, 1996; Moorhouse 1990; Thubron 1994; Whittell 1995).

One obvious explanation for the number of books written about Central Asia derives from political changes in the region, which have meant that it is easier for travellers to get into what Danziger has termed the "forbidden zones." But this is by no means the whole story. Although one aspect of these books is the provision of first-hand information on areas previously difficult to access, it is obvious from the structure of the texts themselves that the authors are seeking to represent themselves as the continuation of the line of nineteenth century travellers to the region. The fascination with Central Asia could therefore arguably be an expression of nostalgia for a lost era, for the end of the Empire, so that in writing about seemingly distant territories, the authors are actually writing about England and her history. The elegiac note in many of the books about Central Asia and the incessant recall of the real and fictitious heroes of the Great Game – Connolly and Stoddart, Bukhara Barnes, Kim, Francis Younghusband – reminds readers that the writers are not just travelling in post-Soviet territories, they are travelling in zones that were once crucial to the British imperial design. Basically, most of these books are adventure stories, and the proliferation of dialogue in them reinforces this view. They are travel books written like novels, full of characters – the ghastly Rosa, Professor at the Academy of Sciences in Kara Kum, who drags Giles Whittell to a dance wearing a diaphanous sixty-five dollar pink suit from Sears in Dayton, Ohio, with matching pink stilettos; the obstructive guides and waiters whom Geoffrey Moorhouse meets in Uzbekistan; Safar who tries laconically to help Colin Thubron find the site of a recent

Turcoman massacre; the Iranian policeman who helps William Dalrymple only after he has, in desperation, produced his Cambridge University card as a form of identification; or the Tibetan who offers Nick Danziger hospitality. One extract from the dialogue between Danziger and the Tibetan serves to illustrate the pace and style of these adventure narratives:

> Our diet on this side trip was limited. Normally, I would happily eat dry raw yak meat, but on one occasion I hesitated. In fact, my stomach turned, for I was offered some really ancient meat, covered with a patina of dust and grime. It looked as if it had been festering in a cupboard for years.
>
> "How old might this be?" I asked tactfully, as one enquiring about the vintage of a wine.
>
> The question pleased the Tibetan. "1983," he said proudly.
>
> "1983?" Horrified!
>
> "November." A true connoisseur.
>
> There was no answer to that. I ate it. I must admit that it tasted just like what it was – vintage, raw yak meat. Dried. I felt that it was even a good year, and a good month.[11]

The ghosts of Sterne and Thackeray and Dickens and Evelyn Waugh haunt many travel writers writing today. Yet these were primarily novelists, while travel writers claim not to be writing fiction, but to be writing truthful accounts of their travels. In other words, the travel writer claims to occupy a position somewhere between that of a journalist and biographer. It is here that the greatest paradox of much contemporary travel writing resides. For while on the one hand, we have the convention of the reporting journalist/author who "tells it like it is," on the other hand we have the obvious manipulation of material for the delight of the readers. One of the most basic examples of the manipulation is the way in which so many travel writers, despite crossing countless linguistic boundaries and their self-confessed ,monolingualism or smattering of one or two languages, nevertheless manage to report lengthy conversations with peasants in the mountains or camel drivers or children from Herat to Kashgar. The moment we pause to ask ourselves in what language might this or that conversation have taken place, we know that we are no longer reading "truthful" accounts, but have stepped across into the realms of fiction.

British Studies and Travel Writing

The study of travel writing deserves to occupy an important place in British Studies for a number of reasons. The very fact of so many travel accounts being written for consumption by British readers from the late eighteenth century to the present deserves our attention. Travel writing, like detective fiction that emerges along a parallel track in roughly the same historical moment, appears to be particularly important to British readers. Both genres involve the reader in a process of hermeneutic exploration, and the question needs to be asked as to why this should be so appealing to British readers and writers.

It is also the case that travel writing relies heavily on stereotypes. The study of stereotypes is central to any form of Area Studies, and again, this is a rich field to explore. The stereotype relies upon a relationship between the Insider and the Other. Understanding the origins of such relationships and the ways in which they continue to dominate is vital in any form of intercultural work. The ways in which travel writers construct images of otherness for a particular readership at a given moment in time need to be mapped out and analyzed.

It would also be important to investigate the differences between

17

styles of travel writing in a diachronic continuum. How great is the contrast between the colonial and post-colonial travel writing traditions, for example? To what extent, we might ask, are the supposedly comic travel books such as those by Nick Danziger or Redmond O'Hanlon a departure from or a continuation of an earlier tradition that does indeed set the culture of readers in a superior position to that of the culture depicted by the writer? And if this is the case, does this explain the success of Bill Bryson in the 1990s, given that whilst his books on the United States and Britain can be said to place both cultures under scrutiny in a position of superiority alongside his readers, his book on Europe is little more than a series of exaggerated, deeply prejudiced, xenophobic sketches?

A study of the historical antecedents of today's travel writing takes us straight into the combined histories of literature on the one hand and society on the other. Travel texts provide an immediate way of accessing a great body of material that might otherwise be impossibly wide to cover. Significantly, a great many travellers deliberately follow the path of travellers from previous times, so there is a strong sense of this kind of writing presenting itself as part of a continuity.

The current fascination with the Central Asian regions, a fascination that has come to the fore in the past decade, provides one example of how travel writers are also intrinsically writing about their own culture even as they purport to be writing about somewhere else. Above all, travel writing can tell us about contacts – how they happen, what takes place in the contact zone. We can learn how cultures construct their image of other cultures, how that image changes (or remains constant through time). Whether we approach the subject from within or without Britain, we will inevitably find our perspectives forced to move. And once we can begin to look differently, we can begin to change.

SUSAN BASSNETT

Notes

1 Felipe Fernandez-Armesto, ed, *Columbus on Himself*, (London: The Folio Society, 1992), 162.

2 Edward Gibbon, in Roger Hudson, ed, *The Grand Tour, 1592-1796*, (London: The Folio Society, 1993), 16-17.

3 Manuel Komroff, ed, *Contemporaries of Marco Polo*, (Consisting of the travel records to the Eastern parts of the world of William of Rubruck, 1253-1255; the journey of John of Pian de Carpini, 1245-1247; and the journal of Friar Odoric, 1318-1330), (London: Cape, 1929).

4 Mary Louise Pratt, *Imperial Eyes: Travel Writing and Transculturation*, (London and New York: Routledge, 1992), 6.

5 Edward Said, *Orientalism*, (New York: Pantheon, 1978), 308.

6 Isabella Bird, *The Yangtze Valley and Beyond: An Account of Journeys in China, Chiefly in the Province of Sze Chuan and Among the Man-Tze of the Somo Territory*, (London: John Murray, 1879; 1880; 1899).

7 William Kinglake, *Eothen: Traces of Travel Brought Home from the East*, (Oxford: Oxford University Press, 1982), 5.

8 Jan Morris, in "Preface" to Kinglake, *Eothen: Traces of Travel Brought Home from the East*, xiv.

9 Bill Bryson, *Notes From a Small Island*, (London and New York: Doubleday, 1995), 11.

10 Bill Bryson, *Notes From a Small Island*, 351-352.

11 Nick Danziger, *Danziger's Travels: Beyond Forbidden Frontiers*, (London: Flamingo, 1988), 336.

References

1 Bann, Stephen, "Travelling to Collect: The Booty of John Bargrave and Charles Waterton," in Robertson et al, 1994, 155-164.

2 Bassnett, Susan, "Grieving for the Great Game: Loss and Englishness in the 1990s" in *From Empire to Multicultural Society: Cultural and Institutional Changes in Britain*, (Würzburg: WVT, 2000).

3 Bird, Isabella, *A Lady's Life in the Rocky Mountains*, (London: John Murray, 1879).

4 Bird, Isabella, *Unbeaten Tracks in Japan: An Account of Travels on Horseback in the Interior Including Visits to the Aborigines of Yezo and the Shrines of Nikko and Ise*, (London: John Murray, 1880).

5 Bird, Isabella, *The Yangtze Valley and Beyond: An Account of Journeys in China, Chiefly in the Province of Sze Chuan and Among the Man-Tze of the Somo Territory*, (London: John Murray, 1899).

19

7   Clavijo, *Embassy to Tamerlaine, 1403-1406*, Translated by Guy Le Strange, (London: George Routledge and Sons, 1928).

8   Bryson, Bill, *Notes From a Small Island*, (London and New York: Doubleday, 1995).

9   Dalrymple, William, *In Xanadu: A Quest*, (London: Harper Collins, 1990).

10   Danziger, Nick, *Danziger's Travels: Beyond Forbidden Frontiers*, (London: Flamingo, 1988).

11   Even-Zohar, Itamar, "The Position of Translated Literature within the Literary Polysystem", in Holmes, Lambert and Van den Broek, 1978.

12   Fernandez-Armesto, Felipe, ed, *Columbus on Himself*, (London: The Folio Society, 1992).

13   Fountaine, Margaret, *Love Among the Butterflies: The Travels and Adventures of a Victorian Lady*, Edited by W F Cater, (London: Collins, 1980).

14   Fountaine, Margaret, *Butterflies and Late Lovers: The Further Travels and Adventures*, Edited by W F Cater, (London: Collins, 1986).

15   Gentzler, Edwin, *Contemporary Translation Theories*, (Clevedon: Multilingual Matters, 1986).

16   Gibbon, Edward, 1993, in Hudson, *The Grand Tour, 1592-1796*, 16-17.

17   Glazebrook, Philip, *Journey to Khiva*, (London: Harvill, 1992).

18   Guin, Ursula Le, *The Left Hand of Darkness*, (New York: Ace, 1969).

19   Hakluyt, R, *The Principal Navigations, Voiages, Traffiques and Discoveries of the English Nation* (Vol.1), (London: Dent, 1907).

20   Holmes, James S, Jose Lambert and Raymond Van den Broek, Editors, *Literature and Translation: New Perspectives*, (Leuven: ACCO, 1978).

21   Hopkirk, Kathleen, *A Traveller's Companion to Central Asia*, (London: John Murray, 1993).

22   Hopkirk, Peter, *The Great Game*, (London: John Murray, 1990).

23   Hopkirk, Peter, *The Quest for Kim: In Search of Kipling's Great Game*, (London: John Murray, 1996).

24   Hudson, Roger, ed, *The Grand Tour, 1592-1796*, (London: The Folio Society, 1993).

25   Kinglake, William, *Eothen: Traces of Travel Brought Home from the East*, (Oxford: Oxford University Press, 1982).

26   Kingsley, Mary, *Travels in West Africa: Congo Français, Corisco and Cameroons*, (London: Macmillan, 1879).

27   Kingsley, Mary, *West African Studies*, (London: Macmillan, 1899).

28   Komroff, Manuel, ed, *Contemporaries of Marco Polo*, (Consisting of the travel records to the Eastern parts of the world of William of Rubruck, 1253-1255; the journey of John of Pian de Carpini, 1245-1247; and the journal of Friar Odoric, 1318-1330), (London: Cape, 1929).

29   Lessing, Doris, *Canopus in Argos: Archives*, (London: Cape, 1979-83).

30   Marquez, Gabriel Garcia, "The Solitude of Latin America" (Nobel Address,
      1982), in McGuirk and Caldwell, 1987, 201-211.

31   McGuirk, Bernard and Richard Caldwell, eds, *Gabriel Garcia Marquez: New
      Reading*, (Cambridge: Cambridge University Press, 1987).

32   Moorhouse, Geoffrey, *Apples in the Snow: A Journey to Samarkand*, (London:
      Hodder and Stoughton, 1990).

33   Morris, Jan, "Preface," in Kinglake, 1982.

34   Plato, *The Republic*, Translated by Desmond Lee, (Harmondsworth: Penguin,
      1974).

35   Polo, Marco, *The Travels of Marco Polo*, Translated by R E Lathan, (Harmondsworth:
      Penguin, 1958).

36   Pratt, Mary Louise, *Imperial Eyes: Travel Writing and Transculturation*, (London and
      New York: Routledge, 1992).

37   Robertson, George et al, eds, *Travellers' Tales: Narratives of Home and Displacement*,
      (London and New York: Routledge, 1994).

38   Said, Edward, *Orientalism*, (New York: Pantheon, 1978).

39   Spurr, David, *The Rhetoric of Empire: Colonial Discourse in Journalism, Travel Writing
      and Imperial Administration*, (Durham and London: Duke University Press, 1993).

40   Suetonius, *History of the Twelve Caesars* (2 volumes), Translated by Phileomon
      Holland, (London: David Nutt, 1899).

41   Sweet, Henry, Editor, "The Voyages of Othere and Wulfstan," *King Alfred's
      Orosius*, (London: Early English Text Society, 1883).

42   Thubron, Colin, *The Lost Heart of Asia*, (London: Heinemann, 1994).

43   Whittell, Giles, *Extreme Continental: Blowing Hot and Cold through Central Asia*,
      (London: Gollancz, 1995).

HAJJI BABA: IDEOLOGICAL BASIS OF THE PERSIAN PICARO

-PALLAVI PANDIT LAISRAM

Anglo-Persian interaction in the nineteenth century resulted in a great number of texts on Persia: the most famous of these was James Morier's "best-seller," *The Adventures of Hajji Baba of Ispahan* (1824). This fast paced picaresque novel/travel account merits close scrutiny in the light of our current knowledge about the discourses of power, particularly Orientalist discourse. Like many other nineteenth century accounts of the Orient, *Hajji Baba* displays a binary view of the world: "good" is Western and Christian and "bad" is Oriental/Persian and Mussalman. *Hajji Baba*, however, moves beyond a simple good/bad division of the world; it also envisions the Orient as a mute, powerless, non-evolving entity which finds a voice only when controlled and improved by the "superior" Western world.

Edward Said, the first major critic to pursue an extended study of Orientalist thought and Orientalist discourse, argued that so pervasive and powerful was Orientalist discourse in the eighteenth and nineteenth centuries, that no one writing on or thinking about the Orient – scientifically, politically or imaginatively – could ignore the large mass of Western works available on the Orient.[1] The writer was conditioned by Orientalism and the Orientalist archive, that is, the large mass of written and unwritten cultural attitudes toward the Orient. As a result, the subject, the Orient, disappeared, and all that remained was works by Orientalists which fed on their own preconceived notions of the Orient.

Although *Hajji Baba* has received considerable academic attention in the twentieth century, its lively style and exciting adventures appear to have obscured, for most literary critics, its visibly Orientalist nature.[2] Art and ideology are, however, closely linked aspects in literature and should not be studied as separate entities. I propose to re-assess the "art" of the novel in the context of its representation of Orientalist discourse. The much praised narrative voice, the "lively" character sketches, and the representation of the picaros within the framework of the picaresque tradition reveal an imaginative control of the inferior, degenerate, frightening, and erotic "other."

It comes as no surprise that a nineteenth century British novel represents an Orientalist vision of the East; what is amazing is the neglect of this aspect of *Hajji Baba* even in the face of James Justinian Morier's well-documented personal sense of alienation from the East. Morier did not initially distance himself from the East: he grew up in Smyrna, and even after being educated in England he returned to Turkey. It was later, during his two diplomatic appointments to Persia, that we see a definite shift from an empathetic to an Orientalist approach to the East.

In 1808 Morier went to Persia in the capacity of private secretary to the envoy, Harford Jones, and wrote one travel account based on this short six-month trip: *A Journey to Persia, Armenia and Asia Minor, to Constantinople, in the Years 1808 and 1809.*[3] In 1810 he went again to Persia, this time elevated to the position of Secretary of the Legation headed by Ambassador Gore Ouseley. He remained in Persia for five years, until 1815, even taking over the reins of diplomatic power after Sir Ouseley's departure in 1814. This second trip culminated in one more travel account, *A Second Journey Through Persia, Armenia and Asia Minor, to Constantinople, in the Years 1810 and 1816.*[4]

The two *Journeys* record a great change in Morier's attitude toward the East. In the first *Journey* we see an empathetic personal approach that treats Persians as individual human beings, mingled with a reductive tendency to stereotype them and a conscious desire to present himself as a contributor to Western scholarly studies of the Orient. In the second *Journey* there is a marked shift towards an Orientalist attitude which sought to study the Orient only to demonstrate or claim Western superiority.

This shift in Morier's perception of the East did not take place in a vacuum. It was closely related to his personal concerns and the political environment he found himself in. Morier's attitude in the first *Journey* was probably more humane because he travelled under the auspices of Harford Jones, a person who had "adopted both the habits and the mores of the people with whom he transacted business."[5] Underlying Morier's humane approach to Persia and the Persians was also the political situation. Jones had been sent to Persia to eliminate the French influence, and in such a situation arrogance was hardly the appropriate attitude. With the French and the British both begging for alliance with Persia, the Persians had the diplomatic edge. Courtesy, respect, and equality were the passwords, and as Morier informs us in *Journey 1808*, even when they were permitted to follow their own inclinations they preferred to follow Persian customs.

Harford Jones' own political problems led to something more than a diplomatic friendship. The then Governor-General of India, Lord Minto, had wanted his favourite, Sir John Malcolm, to be the Envoy to Persia, and he tried to make Jones' Persian mission politically uncomfortable and even dangerous. It was the support of the Persians at this time that made Morier regard them as his "countrymen":

> Throughout the whole management of a new and very delicate situation, their proceedings were *so plain, so upright, and so cheering,* ... that we regarded them with the liveliest gratitude; and felt relieved in finding among strangers all the heart and principle of countrymen.[6] (Emphasis mine).

However, in Morier's second travel account there is a strong consciousness of the East-West difference and a tendency to view the East as a homogenous, alien world: "whatever differences of creed, of government, or of language may exist between them, there is still no line of separation between any two Eastern nations so strong as that which is between Europeans and Asiatics."[7] Morier also expresses a marked sense of Western superiority; he believes that the Persians are "pliable" and "might be entirely civilized" if guided by European nations. Morier's great-niece, Alice Wemyss, has attributed this change in attitude to the loneliness of long residence in a foreign country combined with his isolation from all mission activities due to Sir Ouseley's strange desire to do everything (even the kitchen accounts) all by himself.[8]

The altered political climate, which Morier was aware of as a diplomat, must have also played an important role in the development of this Eurocentric view of the world. A Persian alliance was no longer critically important to the English, while an English alliance had now become vitally important to the Persians (to protect their country from Russian incursions). England had required Persian support as a buffer against France and Russia, but with Napoleon's invasion of Russia in 1812, Russia became an important ally for the British, not an enemy. Consequently Ouseley negotiated the peace treaty of Gulestan (1813) which ceded Persian territories to Russia.

25

The British even rewrote their treaty with Persia, removing those clauses which ensured their help to Persian forces. This awareness of Persian dependence on superior British power was evident to the diplomat Morier who even commented on it in his *Journey 1810*.

In 1817 Morier retired from foreign service (except for a special service in Mexico in 1824) and spent his time recording his experiences in Persia in the form of a fictional narrative by a Persian picaro, *The Adventures of Hajji Baba of Ispahan*. Although written in the form of a picaresque novel, it is clearly based on Morier's experiences in his travels and reflects his intimate knowledge of the customs and practices of Persian society. Along with Hajji we travel to Ispahan, Tehran, Qum, Meshed, the Georgian frontier, Baghdad, and eventually to Constantinople, encountering people from different walks of life: robbers, traders, physicians, soldiers, Christian missionaries, dervishes, mullahs, to name a few. We travel not just through different places, but through many levels of society.

II

A brief survey of the plot of *Hajji Baba* is in order here before we enter into an analysis of Morier's Orientalist vision and its presence in his novel.[9] Hajji, the son of an Ispahani barber, starts life as a naive young man who has never seen the outside world, but longs to be something more than just a barber all his life, for "he had a soul above razors." He accepts a job with Osman Aga because it will give him an opportunity to see life outside Ispahan, but when their caravan is captured by the Turcomans his first act is to steal his master's money because it might be useful in case he succeeds in escaping from the bandits.

Hajji is an innocent boy, naive about the other tricksters in the world, but he does not need anyone to teach him roguery. After he escapes from the Turcomans Hajji becomes a water carrier, but because of a sprained back he shifts to tobacco selling.

26

Unfortunately, to make a quick profit, Hajji starts selling adulterated tobacco, for which he gets punished by the officers of the law. After this he becomes a dervish, a teller of traditional folk tales in this case, but when he accidentally runs into a messenger carrying the court poet's letter to his family, he steals the letter and the messenger's horse, and delivers the letter himself in the hope of a reward. When the poet returns home he begs of him some kind of employment, and the poet obliges, placing him in the royal physician's service. But Hajji wearies of working for the physician because he sees no future in it, and he requests the doctor to recommend him to the chief executioner to replace an officer who had died recently.

As an officer, Hajji is up to mischief again because his comrade, Shir Ali, "gave me such an insight into the advantages of the situation, that I could dream of nothing but bastinadoing and getting money."[10] Hajji soon has to leave this job and run for his life for having seduced Zeenab, one of the inmates of the Shah's harem, but ultimately after living for some time as a holy man in the protection of a religious sanctuary, he obtains the Shah's pardon. But soon after he engages in illegal work, arranging temporary marriages, or in other words dealing in prostitution, until finally, when his ill doings lead to the harassment of the Christians, the Shah expels him from Tehran. Partly through luck and partly by connivance Hajji steals a horse and some money and crosses the frontier into Turkey. Here, with the help of Osman Aga, his first master, he sets up a business, but his greed, and vanity, and deceit, soon bring him down, and penniless he turns to the Persian Ambassador who offers him a job.

By the time Morier wrote *Hajji Baba* his immense knowledge of many facets of life in Persia was strongly infused with the Orientalist perception of the East as an inferior, degenerate, erotic place which requires the guiding light of Western civilization. The very style of the novel – the narrative voice, the character portrayal, and the depiction of the picaros within the picaresque form – imaginatively

27

dominates Persia and represents it as an object, inferior, mute and ridiculous. The real narrator is not the Persian but the Englishman hiding behind the Persian mask, presenting us a reductive Eurocentric view of an Orient that finds expression only through the intervention and mediation of the Western world.

This English voice views all Persian characters as flat, unchanging beings, reflecting its vision of the stereotypical roguish, decadent, erotic Oriental. The picaresque form is of course a useful literary convention for displaying such individuals; however, in Morier's hands it becomes a technique for depicting his perception of the *inherent* failings of the Persian/Eastern character. As we shall see, Morier has been very selective about his picaros: "good" is Western or Christian, and "bad" is Persian and Mussalman.

In the fictional introductory epistle to the novel we are informed that Hajji is the author, the narrative voice of the novel, whereas the Englishman, Peregrine is the editor. Hajji explains to Peregrine that he maintained a record of his life because

> Ever since I have known your nation [the English] I have remarked their inquisitiveness and eagerness after knowledge. Whenever I have travelled with them, I observed they record their observations in books; and when they return home, thus make their fellow country-men acquainted with the most distant regions of the globe. Will you believe me, that I, Persian as I am, have followed their example; and that during the period of my residence at Constantinople, I have passed my time in writing a detailed history of my life, ...[11]

Underlying Hajji's explanation is the image of a mute Persia, unable to represent itself unless touched and improved by the West. Had Hajji not been inspired by the world that seeks knowledge, he, "Persian" that he is, would not have seen any need to express his thoughts about his life and adventures. And even then his portrayal of his country would be incomprehensible to the Western audience unless, according to Peregrine, a Westerner edited it for "European readers, divesting it of the numerous repetitions, and the tone of exaggeration and hyperbole which pervade the compositions of Easterners."[12]

We soon realize that the narrative voice is only theoretically Hajji's. Even though the tale is narrated in the first person by Hajji, there are important sequences that allow the reader to realize that he is no more than a puppet on an English string. For example, to backtrack a bit, Hajji's comment that Persian though he is, he wrote about his life sounds most unnatural because he is referring to himself not as an individual but as a representative of a country. Hajji does this quite often in the novel claiming that he is heartless or vain because he is a Persian or because he is a Mussalman. When he tries to overcome his sorrow at his separation from Zeenab, he talks as though he is a representative Mussalman: "I endeavoured ... to show myself a true Mussalman by my contempt for woman kind."[13] He also describes his own vanity as a Persian failing: "the ninety five pieces of gold in my girdle ... made it difficult for me to restrain that vanity of display so common to all my countrymen."[14] Behind the so-called first person we hear the real voice, the voice of the Westerner interpreting Persia and Islam for us.

Morier's half-concealed voice also emerges in inconsistencies in the narrative voice to give us its picture of Persian character. For example, in the description of the chaoush (guide) who was to escort their caravan from Tehran to Meshed, Hajji says that the chaoush was a "character well known on the road between Tehran and Meshed, and enjoyed a reputation for courage, which he had acquired for having cut off a Turcoman's head whom he had found dead on the road."[15] How could Hajji have known that the chaoush had cut off a dead man's head? He had just arrived in Tehran from Ispahan, and was a naive boy, away from home for the first time. It is through asides like these, placed in Hajji's mouth, that Morier presents a so-called "realistic" Persian commentary on cowardly Persians.

Under the guise of first person narration, the guise of realism and authenticity, we are presented a Eurocentric "realism," that is, what the Western world chose to define as authentically Oriental. Morier's Western voice is so obvious that one wonders why it has not been noticed before. Perhaps such a state of affairs exists because Western scholars like Wallace Cable Brown would unconsciously endorse Morier's perspective, and therefore would not question his subtle, and often unsubtle, intrusions.[16]

Morier also portrays characters in a manner which reflects his Western orientation to the East. To the Western world, the Orient was just one imaginary entity, different and inferior, and it could not see the Orient as composed of people of various traits and personalities. Consequently, although they observed the Orientals in minute detail, they ultimately reduced them to objects, to stereotypical beings who can have no individual life history or development, but are merely "specimens." It was as though the Western observers could not cope with this alien world unless they fitted it into some preconceived category. Morier, in spite of his personal experiences in the Orient too tends to reduce his characters to types which embody the Western notion of Orientals.

Hajji himself appears to be an embodiment of Western notions of the static, unchanging East, of that "singularly unchanging Oriental people," as Lord Curzon said in his introduction to the 1895 edition of the novel.[17] Hajji embodies this quality in the essentially unchanging nature of his character. We see him through various adventures, trials and tribulations, we see him as a young boy just starting out in life, and finally as secretary to the Persian Ambassador, but we see no change in his personality. He starts life as a vain young man and as a rogue, and when we last see him he is still vain and roguish, but much older. Even though he sees examples of "noble" Englishmen, he remains the same, thus fulfilling the expectations of the Orientalist C J Wills that "Persia does not change."[18]

The other characters in Hajji Baba do not develop a life of their own even though they either narrate their own life histories and/or are described by other Persians in the novel. Two such notable characters are Zeenab and Sefer who embody Western stereotypes of Eastern sexuality and decadent religious beliefs.

Dervish Sefer's account of his life and adventures contains only incidents that pertain to the fraudulent nature of dervishes. And his manner of referring to dervishes in the plural pronoun further reduces any trace of individuality: he sprinkles his entire dialogue with "us" dervishes, and "we,' and "our." Sefer's individuality is reduced to such an extent that he even becomes the spokesman for Western attitudes toward Islam. The success of Islam was very threatening to the Western world (this sense of threat can be seen in English literature as early as in the sixteenth century and well into the nineteenth century) because its very basis challenged and superseded their religion, and one of their ways of coping with it was by attributing the Prophet's success to cunning and trickery. According to Sefer, or rather according to Morier, Sefer says that "[I]f I chose to give myself the trouble, and incur the risks which Mahomed himself did, I might even now become as great a prophet as he."[19] Sefer has no life of his own, he has merely become a specimen in a Western sociological laboratory, studied by a scientist who first forms his conceptions of the object and then in a "realistic" manner applies it.

Zeenab, Hajji's beloved, conveys a different kind of Western image of the Orient, that of the sexually appealing Oriental woman:

> Her blue veil was negligently thrown over her head; and as she stooped, the two long tresses which flowed from her forehead

hung down in so tantalising a manner as nearly to screen all her face ... Her hands were small ... her feet were equally small; and her whole air and form bespoke loveliness and grace ... [she] had the most enchanting features that the imagination can conceive ... At this moment she let her veil fall, as if by chance, and I had time to look upon her face, which was even more beautiful than I had imagined. Her eyes were large and peculiarly black, and fringed by long lashes, which ... formed a sort of ambuscade from which she levelled her shafts ... Her sweet nose was aquiline, her mouth small and full of sweet expression ... Nothing could equal the beauty of her hair; it was black as jet and fell in long tresses down her back.[20]

The picture of Zeenab conveys the Western image of the mysteriously veiled Eastern woman who conceals her charms, her sensuous and enchanting features, behind her drapery. She is not only a sexual object whose tresses "tantalisingly" screen her face, but she is also a sexually uninhibited person who "levels her shafts" and who drops her veil "as if by chance." Zeenab represents the sexually dangerous and exciting image of the Orient and the Oriental woman.

III

The characters in *Hajji Baba* should also be studied in the context of the picaresque form of the novel. Morier wrote *Hajji Baba* in the picaresque form, and he naturally made his central character, Hajji, a picaro. Hajji's characterization raises a few questions. Is Hajji a rogue simply because he is a character in a picaresque novel, or is he a rogue also because Morier considered all Persians to be rascals? Does Morier portray the Persians and Mussalmans in the novel as picaros because of the conventions of the form he was using, or did he do so because he felt that "Oriental" and "picaro" are synonymous concepts? To explore this aspect of the novel we must first define the picaresque form and also survey the picaresque novel, *The Adventures of Gil Blas of Santillane*, that Morier borrowed from considerably.[21]

The concept of the picaresque novel has undoubtedly undergone changes over the years, but what concerns us here are some of the essential elements of this technique. Monteser and Miller have identified some of the basic elements of this category of literature.[22] According to Monteser, the picaro must be of the lower classes, a rogue and not a villain, and "must be conscious, either during his adventures or later as a mature author, of the reflections upon society which his tale points up. He need not criticize it, but he must be aware of what the reader is to criticize."[23] Miller explores the character of the rogue further, arguing that the picaro is a "relative innocent developing into a picaro because the world he meets is roguish."[24]

Hajji Baba, which Monteser has classified as a picaresque novel, by and large fits the above description. However, there are important variations to Morier's use of the picaresque, and variations from his avowed model, Le Sages's *The Adventures of Gil Blas of Santillane*, which reveal that Morier was making a Eurocentric comment on the people he was writing about.

In *Hajji Baba* Morier portrays a picaro who is leading a life of roguery because he wants to, and not merely because the world he meets is "roguish." Hajji is not a "relative innocent" who develops into a rogue: he is inherently a rogue. The summary of Hajji's adventures presented earlier in the paper demonstrates this clearly. Hajji travels from place to place and keeps changing occupations out of ambition or monetary considerations. Very often he has to be on the move because of his own illegal or mischievous activities. The picaro is in this particular case not corrupt because of the nature of the society around him; even when he is away from the corrupting influence of court life, working among honest merchants, he continues with his tricks. It is this deviation from the development of the picaro in a picaresque world that leads one to conclude that it was Morier's deliberate intention to demonstrate what he regarded as the inherently decadent nature of the Persians. The picaresque form was ideal for Morier because while it enabled him to depict a chaotic world and to survey its rogues, a slight, but important, change in the genre also permitted him to represent his conception of the ethical inferiority of the Orientals.

Hajji's immaturity and lack of growth also distinguishes him from the traditional picaro, and this deviation too reveals the Western assumption of cultural superiority. A picaresque novel, as defined earlier, is written by a mature narrator who, even if he does not criticize his society, at least knows what there is to criticize. Hajji, however, is far from mature, and he never looks back and comments on his society. Only once, when he observes that he is not cruel by nature but has become hardhearted by the example of the other nasakchi's (officer attached to the chief executioner, or bailiff), does he imply a comment on the brutality of the society. Generally speaking, Hajji is content to describe events in a deadpan tone, neither implying criticism, nor directly commenting on the nature of the incident he is presenting to us. Even when he makes remarks on the "Persians," as mentioned earlier, he does not intend any criticism. Hajji may comment on the envy and malevolence of the Persian, but it is not a moral issue for him because he revels in this kind of behaviour and he deliberately tries to make other people jealous because it makes him feel important.

Hajji is obviously a very different character from Gil Blas who observes and comments on the ills of his society, and ultimately retreats from it completely. Morier borrowed considerably from *Gil Blas* – both themes and incidents – and therefore any significant change in the narrative of *Hajji Baba* is worth noticing.[25] The alterations that Morier made in the presentation of the rogues is particularly important because it reveals his conscious intention of demonstrating that the vices he is presenting are specifically Oriental and Islamic, and definitely not English/European or Christian.

When Le Sage exposes the vices of his society, he often does so by presenting an ideal in the form of an individual, or a critic, from within that same community. In *Gil Blas* we witness corrupt doctors and ministers, but we also see doctors who critique the corrupt among them, and noble lords who use their influence to protect their friends from corrupt ministers. Dr Sangrado, the incompetent, unethical, and comical doctor, is mocked by Dr Cuchillo who even gets into a fight with the doctor's apprentice, Gil Blas. And for all the corrupt officers we meet at court, particularly the Duke of Lerma, prime minister to the Spanish Crown, we are presented with a counterbalance in the Lords of Leyva who consistently assist Gil Blas. For all the Sirenas we also have the virtuous wives, Seraphina, Antonia, Beatrice, and Dorothea.

Morier's narrative, however, consists of a series of oppositions between Westerners and Christians on the one hand, and Persians and Muslims on the other hand, which serves to make it very clear that these vices are connected with origin and religion, not the socio-economic and political conditions of a Persian's life. Moreover, although these faults and vices of greed, hypocrisy, and deceit are universal in nature (as Weinberger and Grabar observe), Morier presents them not only as essentially Persian in nature, but also as absent in English and Christians.

The pairs of contrasts that the narrative sets up demonstrate that the vices are indeed "foreign" to a superior Western, Christianized culture. Hasan Javadi, analyzes one such contrast: the "parallel stories" of Zeenab and Hajji, and Yusuf and his Mariam.[26] Zeenab gladly leaves her lover when a better opportunity presents itself, whereas Mariam, risking her life, escapes to her lover; and as for the two men, Yusuf risks his life to save Mariam, even keeps his oath to Hajji, a Mussalman, whereas Hajji, although deeply troubled, does nothing to save Zeenab, and even participates in the death of Zeenab and his own child. The Christians alone possess the values of loyalty, love truthfulness, and of course ultimately gain the reward of a safe and secure life.

There are other pairs too: Mollah Nadan and the Frank dervish, and Mirza Ahmak and the Frank physician. Mollah Nadan is a fanatic and a rogue, trying to make himself more important than the Mollah Bashi, and of course attempting to make as much money as possible by arranging temporary marriages. The corrupt Mollah may be a stock figure "within the oriental scene, in puppet pantomime" as Grabar argues, and the image of the corrupt man of religion is, as Weinberger states, a universal one, but in *Hajji Baba* the Mollah is not merely a traditional or universal figure but, instead, a contrast to the courageous and intelligent Frank dervish. The Mollah himself informs us that the Frank was "of a wit so sharp, that the Shaitan in person was not fit to be his father. His eyes were like live charcoal, and his voice like a high wind. He never lost an opportunity of entering into an argument with our most learned men ... with the heart of a lion ..."[27] This apostolic Frank dervish's actions too reveal him to be a very capable and rational man who can stand his ground and reason with a mob of Mussalmans intent on harassing him. Mollah Nadan clearly does not embody the universal image of the corrupt priest: he embodies the corruption of the Mussalman clergy.

Mirza Ahmak, the royal physician, is presented as a contrast to the two Frank doctors in Persia. It is not just that the Mirza's knowledge is limited compared to the "modern" science of the Franks, but his attitude toward his patients is also highly unethical. He is annoyed that the Franks have invented a vaccine for small pox because "[t]he small pox had always been a comfortable source of revenue to me; I cannot afford to lose it because an infidel chooses to come here and treat us like cattle."[28] The Frank doctors, on the other hand, not only treat their patients gratis, they also believe that "the blessing [the vaccine] must be spread throughout the world."[29] Persian and Mussalman ethics are thus immediately labelled as inferior to the supposedly altruistic Western culture which was currently making Persia a pawn of European power politics. The Eurocentric view of the world never sees anything as universal because it never judges itself by the same standard it applies to the Orient, and since Morier's narrative of cultural contrasts eliminates any hint of universality it endorses this attitude.

Morier seems unable to present good, loyal, generous Persians and Turks; and even when he does so he glosses over them so fast that they are not noticed, or sometimes he deliberately, as an afterthought, distorts their personalities, abruptly reducing them to comic or avaricious figures. Among the good characters who get glossed over are the kind muleteer, the cadi (police officer-cum-magistrate), and the Mollah who rescues the Frank dervish. The characters who suffer distortion are the Turk Osman Aga, Hajji's mother and his schoolmaster. Obviously, Morier has been very selective about his picaros: "good" is Western or Christian, and "bad" is Persian and Mussalman.

IV

Many literary critics choose to ignore the Orientalist discourse represented in this novel. These scholars like to remind us that the Persians enjoyed *Hajji Baba* in its Persian translation. While the translation of *Hajji Baba* is not the main topic of discussion in this paper, it is an important, closely related issue which must be addressed.

If the novel is a sample of Western conceptions of the Orient, as has been argued, why did the Persians enjoy it, and why did they perceive it to be satiric? I am unable to read Persian, but Hassan

Kamshad's summary of the omissions and transformations made by the translator provide some clues that can help answer the question.[30]

Hassan Kamshad notes that the extended Mariam-Yusuf tale, which runs parallel to the Hajji-Zeenab relationship was shortened to a mere five pages in the translation. Moreover, instead of referring to Persian officials by their ranks, as Morier did, the translator refers to them by their actual names or titles.

The abridgement of the Mariam-Yusuf story makes a vast difference to the intent of the translation. The Mariam-Yusuf story in the original follows Zeenab's joyful departure to the Shah's harem, and develops with Mariam's escape from the Governor's palace, concludes with Yusuf's courageous rescue of Mariam and his family, which is soon followed by Hajji's cowardly self-preservation and Zeenab's death. The tale is clearly intended as a contrast between good Christian behaviour, and that of typical self-serving, Mussalman lovers. To compress this tale is to mitigate the implied comments, and to probably also disturb the sequence of events, a sequence which highlights the contrast between Christianity and Islam.

The other change is the most important of all because it is this, which makes the novel a political satire, not a document attesting Western superiority. By changing the references to officials in *Hajji Baba of Ispahan* to recognizable, well known, corrupt politicians, the translator was commenting not on the nature of Persians, but on the characters of specific, notorious individuals. Thus we now have a novel, written by a Persian, and directed toward a Persian audience, because only a Persian audience would recognize the figures being satirized. The British-Persian contrasts in the novel would cease to be comments on Persian culture, and instead become a criticism of specific individuals.

The Persians themselves viewed the book as a political satire for, according to Phillot (the British Consul in Kerman), the Persians appreciated "the skill with which their countryman had depicted certain notable characters."[31] It was only when "the English original reached me [Phillot] from India, ... [that] *Haji* [sic] *Baba* ceased to be popular," because the Persians now realized the true intent of the book. Phillot's reference to a Persian's reaction to the English version shows this new awareness: "the author has overstepped his bounds; he has made fun of everyone from the Shah downwards."[32] The Orientalist aspects of *Hajji Baba* clearly cannot be wished away by reference to the success of the Persian translation.

Hajji Baba is undoubtedly a fast-paced, exciting narrative, full of characters whose foolish behaviour and unethical conduct is comical in their innocent acceptance of it. However, we must not be insensitive to the attitudes underlying the novel, nor to the attitudes that we reflect when we find it comical. To do so would be to ignore the individuality and humanity of the people it describes, and from a literary standpoint, a failure to see the relationship between form and content.

Hajji Baba's popularity continued well into the first half of the twentieth century, thus demonstrating not only Morier's skill as a writer, but also the extent to which the Western world unconsciously endorsed his vision of Orientals. Unfortunately, educated Oriental readers have a tendency to imitate Western attitudes: "One wonders why such a delightful book should have been saddled with such ethnological, cultural or political interpretations," writes Moussa-Mahmoud.[33] The purpose of this analysis is not to denigrate the artistic value of this book, but to sensitize both the Western and the Oriental reader to the reductive and offensive aspects of the text. Readers should be able to enjoy this novel, and many others of its kind, but at the same time develop an understanding of the ways in which it can offend cultural sensibilities. A meaningful, non-hegemonic, cross-cultural dialogue can take place only when individuals can sympathetically "travel" into the thoughts and feelings of another culture.

Notes

1   Edward Said, *Orientalism*, (New York: Vintage Books, 1979).
2   Wallace Cable Brown, "Prose Fiction and English Interest in the Near East, 1775-1825," PMLA 53, 1938: 827-836.
    Ava Inez Weinberger, "The Middle Eastern Writings of James Morier: Traveller, Novelist and Creator of Hajji Baba," Dissertation, University of Toronto, 1984.
    Terry Harris Grabar, "*Hajji Baba of Ispahan*: A Critical Study," Dissertation, University of Michigan, 1962.
3   James Morier, *A Journey Through Persia, Armenia and Asia Minor, to Constantinople, in the years 1808 and 1809*, (London: Longman, 1812).
4   James Morier, *A Second Journey Through Persia, Armenia and Asia Minor, to Constantinople, in the Years 1810 and 1816. With a Journal of the Voyage By the Brazils and Bombay to the Persian Gulf. Together With An Account of the Proceedings of His Majesty's Embassy Under His Excellency Sir Gore Ouseley*, (London: Longman, 1818).
5   Alice Wemyss, "The Birth of Hajji Baba as Seen Through the Letters of James Morier," Persica 7, 1978: 165-72. In *An Account of the Transactions of His Majesty's Mission to the Court of Persia in the Years 1807-11*, Jones writes, "[H]e who attempts to make us believe that the inhabitants of Persia and the Persian peasantry, are, in moral character the same, knows little or nothing of what he is talking about, and he who imagines that the Persian peasants of Fars, Irak, Azarbaijan, or any other province, all possess the same moral qualities, is equally ignorant" (92).
6   James Morier, *Journey, 1810*, 220.
7   James Morier, *Journey, 1810*, viii.
8   Alice Wemyss, "The Birth of Hajji Baba as Seen Through the Letters of James Morier," 1978, 170.
9   James Morier, *The Adventures of Hajji Baba of Ispahan*, Ed., C J Wills, (London: Lawrence and Bullen, 1897). All page references to *Hajji Baba* in this study will be from C J Wills' 1897 edition.
10 James Morier, *The Adventures of Hajji Baba of Ispahan*, 227.
11 James Morier, *The Adventures of Hajji Baba of Ispahan*, xviia.
12 James Morier, *The Adventures of Hajji Baba of Ispahan*, xviia.
13 James Morier, *The Adventures of Hajji Baba of Ispahan*, 314.
14 James Morier, *The Adventures of Hajji Baba of Ispahan*, 479.
15 James Morier, *The Adventures of Hajji Baba of Ispahan*.
16 Wallace Cable Brown, "Prose Fiction and English Interest in the Near East, 1775-1825," PMLA 53, 1938: 835.
17 Lord Curzon of Kedlestone, Introduction, *The Adventures of Hajji Baba of Ispahan*, by James Morier (London: Macmillan, 1895).
18 Preface to 1897 edition of *Hajji Baba*.

19 James Morier, *Hajji Baba*, 61.

20 James Morier, 137-139.

21 Alain-Rene Le Sage, *The Adventures of Gil Blas of Santillane*, Translated by Tobias Smollet, (Oxford: Oxford University Press, 1937).

22 Frederick Monteser, *The Picaresque Element in Western Literature*, Studies in the Humanities 5 (Alabama: University of Alabama Press, 1975).
    Stuart Miller, *The Picaresque Novel* (Cleveland: Case Western Reserve University Press, 1967).

23 Frederick Monteser, *The Picaresque Element in Western Literature*, 3.

24 Stuart Miller, *The Picaresque Novel*, 56.

25 See Terry H Grabar's "*Hajji Baba of Ispahan*: A Critical Study," 1962, Ava Inez Weinberger's "The Middle Eastern Writings of James Morier: Traveller, Novelist and Creator of Hajji Baba," 1984, and Hasan Javadi's "James Morier and his Hajji Baba of Ispahan," 1970, for extensive details on the similarities between *Gil Blas* and *Hajji Baba*.

26 Hasan Javadi, "James Morier and his Hajji Baba of Ispahan," *Iran Society Silver Jubilee Souvenir* 1944-1969, (Calcutta: Iran Society, 1970), 171.

27 James Morier, *Hajji Baba*, 462.

28 James Morier, *Hajji Baba*, 116.

29 James Morier, *Hajji Baba*, 571.

30 Hassan Kamshad, "New Lights on the Translation of Hajji Baba Isfahani" *Persica* 1, 1963-64: 70-75.

31 D C Phillot, Introduction, *The Adventures of Hajji Baba of Ispahan*, by James Morier, translated by Shaikh Ahmad-Ikirmani (Calcutta: Asiatic Society of Bengal, 1905), ix.

32 D C Phillot, Introduction, ix.

33 Fatma Moussa-Mahmoud, "Orientals in Picaresque: A Chapter in the History of the Oriental Tale in England," *Cairo Studies in English*, 145-188, (1961-62), 174.

41

POROUS BOUNDARIES AND CULTURAL CROSSOVER: FANNY PARKES AND "GOING NATIVE"

WILLIAM DALRYMPLE

W e are rather oppressed just now by a lady, Mrs Parkes, who insists on belonging to our camp," wrote Emily Eden in December 1837.

"She has a husband who always goes mad in the cold season, so she says it is her duty to herself to leave him and travel about. She has been a beauty and has remains of it, and is abundantly fat and lively. At Benares, where we fell in with her she informed us she was an Independent Woman."

Emily Eden was the sister of the Governor General, Lord Auckland, and the First Lady of British India. Fanny Parkes was the wife of a mentally unstable junior official in charge of ice making in Allahabad. The different status of the two women made friendship between the two impossible, and posterity has been far kinder to Emily than it has been to Fanny: Eden's *Up the Country* has long been regarded as one of the great classics of British Imperial literature and rarely been out of print since it was first published in 1866 – the critic Lord David Cecil went as far as placing the author "in the first flight of English women letter writers." In comparison Fanny Parkes's *Wanderings of a Pilgrim in Search of the Picturesque* had no second edition, and has only recently been reprinted, and that in an expensive two volume academic edition. In contrast to the fame of Emily Eden, few have ever heard of Fanny Parkes. Fewer still have read her.

Yet anyone who today reads the work of these two women together can hardly fail but to prefer Fanny's writing to that of her more famous contemporary. While Emily is witty and intelligent but waspish, haughty and conceited, Fanny is an enthusiast and an eccentric with a burning love of India that imprints itself on almost every page of her book. From her first arrival in Calcutta, she writes how "I was charmed by the climate; the weather was delicious; and I thought India a most delightful country ... could I have gathered around me the dear ones I had left in England, my happiness would have been complete." The initial intuition was only reinforced the longer she stayed in South Asia. In the twenty four years she lived in India, the country never ceased to surprise, intrigue and delight her, and she was never happier than when off on another journey under canvas exploring new parts of the country: "Oh the pleasure," she writes, "of vagabondizing in India!"

It was partly the sheer beauty of the country that hypnotized her. Indian men she found "remarkably handsome," while her response to Indian nature was no less admiring: "The evenings are cool and refreshing ... The foliage of the trees, so luxuriously beautiful and so novel is to me a source of constant admiration." But it was not just the way the place looked. The longer she stayed in India, the more Fanny grew to be fascinated by the culture, history, flowers, trees, religions, languages and peoples of the country, the more she felt possessed by an overpowering urge just to pack her bags and set off and explore: "With the Neapolitan saying, 'Vedi Napoli, e poi mori,' I beg to differ entirely," she wrote, "and would rather offer *this* advice, – 'See the Taj Mahal, and then – see the Ruins of Delhi.' How much there is to delight the eye in this bright, this beautiful world! Roaming about with a good tent and a good Arab [horse], one might be happy for ever in India."

It is this sheer joy, excitement and even liberation in travel that Fanny Parkes manages so well to communicate. In the same way, it is her wild, devil-may-care enthusiasm, insatiable curiosity and love of the country that immediately engages the reader and carries him or her with Fanny as she bumbles her way across India on her own, wilfully dismissive of the dangers of dacoits or thugs or tigers, learning the sitar, enquiring about the intricacies of Hindu mythology, trying opium, taking down recipes for scented tobacco, talking her way into harems, befriending Maratha princesses and collecting Hindu statuary, fossils, butterflies, zoological specimens preserved in spirits, Indian aphorisms and Persian proverbs – all with an unstoppable, gleeful excitement. Even when she dislikes a particular Indian custom, she often finds herself engaged intellectually. Watching the Churuk Puja, or "hook swinging," when pious Hindus attached hooks into the flesh of their backs and were swung about on ropes hanging from great cranes for the amusement of the crowds below, "some in penance for their own sins, some for those of others, richer men, who reward their deputies and thus do penance by proxy," Fanny wrote that: "I was much disgusted, but greatly interested."

Moreover the longer she stayed in India, the more Fanny became slowly Indianized. The professional memsahib, herself the daughter of a colonial official (Captain William Archer), who came to India to watch over her colonial administrator husband, was gradually transformed into a fluent Urdu speaker, who spent less and less of her time at her husband's *mofussil* posting, and more and more of her time travelling around to visit her Indian friends. Aesthetically she grew slowly to prefer Indian dress to that of the English. At one point watching Id celebrations at the Taj she notes how

> Crowds of gaily dressed and most picturesque natives were seen in all directions passing through the avenue of fine trees, and by the side of the fountains to the tomb: they added great beauty to the scene, whilst the eye of taste turned away pained and annoyed by the vile round hats and stiff attire of the European gentlemen, and the equally ugly bonnets and stiff and graceless dresses of the English ladies.

Later, visiting the women in Colonel Gardner's Khasgunge zenana, she again praises Indian ways over those of Europe:

> [Mulka Begum] walks very gracefully, and is as straight as an arrow. In Europe how rarely – how very rarely – does a woman walk gracefully! Bound up in stays, the boy as stiff as a lobster in a shell; that snake-like undulating movement – the poetry of motion – is lost, destroyed by the stiffness of the waist and hip, which impedes free movement of the limbs. A lady in European attire gives me the idea of a German manikin; an Asiatic, in her flowing drapery, recalls the statues of antiquity.

She can barely believe the philistinism of the Government in Calcutta and recoils in horror when she sees what the English have done to the beautifully inlaid Mughal zenana apartments in the Agra Fort:

> Some wretches of European officers – to their disgrace be it said – made this beautiful room a cook-room! And the ceiling, the fine marbles, and the inlaid work, are all one mass of blackness and defilement! Perhaps they cooked the su'ar, the hog, the unclean beast, within the sleeping apartments of Noor-Jahan – the proud, the beautiful Sultana!

45

Even more angry is her response when she hears that the Turkish

> Baths in the apartments below the palace, which most
> probably belonged to the zenana, were broken up by the
> Marquis of Hastings: he committed this sacrilege of the
> past ... [Then] having destroyed the beauty of the baths of the
> palace, the remaining marble was afterwards sold on account
> of the Government; most happily the auction brought so
> small a sum, it put a stop to further depredations.

Gradually, over the twenty four years she lived in India, and as her *Wanderings* took shape, Fanny's views begin to change. Having assumed at first that good taste is the defining characteristic of European civilization and (especially that of her own people,) she finds her assumptions being challenged by what she comes to regard as the rampant philistinism of the English in India, and by the beauty of so much of Indian life, not least its architecture. (In this, incidentally, she would have agreed with Robert Byron who was equally horrified by what the English had done to India a hundred years later: "In a country full of good example," he wrote, "the English have left the mark of the beast." He also wrote with horror about "how the whole of [British] India is a gigantic conspiracy to make one imagine one is in Balham or Eastbourne ... [as for Darjeeling] imagine Bognor or Southend roofed in corrugated iron and reassembled in the form of an Italian hill town ...")

Every bit as bad, in Fanny's eyes, was the attitude of the British who employed a band at the Taj so that visiting Company officials could have the opportunity to dance a jig on the marble platform in front of the tomb: "Can you imagine anything so detestable?" she wrote.

> European ladies and gentlemen dance quadrilles in front of
> the tomb! I cannot enter the Taj without feelings of deep
> devotion: the sacredness of the place, the remembrance of

the fallen grandeur of the family of the Emperor, the solemn echoes, the dim light, the beautiful architecture, the exquisite finish and delicacy of the whole ... all produce deep and sacred feelings; and I could no more jest or indulge in levity beneath the dome of the Taj, than I could in my prayers.

On leaving the enclosure, she writes, movingly:

And now adieu! Beautiful Taj – adieu! In the far, far West I shall rejoice that I have gazed upon your beauty; nor will the memory depart until the lowly tomb of an English gentlewoman closes on my remains.

Over time, these emotional and aesthetic responses to India slowly consolidated themselves into something more structured, and in due course they clearly profoundly altered Fanny's political outlook. By the late 1830's she came to be increasingly critical of the East India Company her husband served. In her published work that criticism was by necessity muted, but her allegiances are clear. At a time when many of her contemporaries were calling for the British to annex the "degenerate" Kingdom of Oude (or Avadh as it is more usually spelled today) Fanny was quite clear that, "the subjects of his Majesty of Oude are by no means desirous of participating in the blessings of British rule. They are a richer, sleeker, and merrier race than the natives in the territories of the Company." She rails against the authorities for failing to reward her friend William Gardner for his gallantry (largely, though she does not say this, because of the degree to which Gardner was believed to have "gone native" by the "rulers of the land" as Fanny calls them.) She points out how many have died painful, unnecessary deaths from smallpox as "Lord William Bentinck did away with the vaccine department, to save a few rupees; from which economy many have lost their lives."

At the end of her travels, when Fanny finally looks forward to seeing her family in England again, she turns to a Persian aphorism to express the intensity of her feelings: "The desire of the garden never leaves the heart of the nightingale." Yet when she finally sets foot on English soil again, her return is not a moment for rejoicing but for depression and disappointment:

> We arrived at 6 am. May flowers and sunshine were in my thoughts. [But instead ...] it was bitterly cold walking up from the boat – rain wind and sleet, mingled together, beat on my face. Every thing on landing was so wretchedly mean, especially the houses, which are built of slate stone, and also slated down the side; it was cold and gloomy ... I felt a little disgusted.

When she arrived home, her mother barely recognized her. It was as if the current of colonization has somehow been reversed: the colonizer had been colonized. India had changed and transformed Fanny Parkes. She could never be the same again.

In 1822 when Fanny Parkes arrived in India, British attitudes to the country were undergoing a major transformation.

In the late eighteenth century, the more intelligent of the British in India tended to respond to their adopted country with amazement and fascination. Under the influence of Sir William Jones, the Chief Justice of the new Supreme Court at Calcutta, there was a sudden explosion of interest for what Jones called "this wonderful country." In 1784, Jones had founded an Asiatik Society "for inquiring into the History, Civil and Natural, the Antiquities, Arts, Sciences and Literature of Asia." Its patron was the most enlightened of all the British Governor Generals, Warren Hastings, who shared the new enthusiasm for Hinduism and who declared "in truth I love India a little more than my own country." Under Jones and Hastings, the Royal Asiatic Society quickly became the catalyst for a sudden explosion of interest in Hinduism, as it formed enduring relations with the local Bengali intelligentsia and led the way to uncovering the deepest roots of Indian history and civilization. In India, Jones wrote that he had discovered Arcadia. Valmiki was the new Homer, the Ramayana the new Odyssey. The possibilities seemed endless.

Yet in the early years of the nineteenth century, this optimism and excitement began to wane, and senior figures in the Company began to become openly disdainful of all things Indian. Partly the reasons for this were political. In the eighteenth century the Company was a small, vulnerable coastal power that depended on the goodwill of Indian rulers. Many Indian armies were better equipped and better trained than those of the Company: the armies of Tipu Sultan for example had rifles and canon which were based on the latest French designs, and their artillery had a heavier bore and longer range than anything possessed by the Company's armies. But by the 1830's, having defeated Tipu Sultan and the Marathas, the British had become the paramount power in India. For the first time there was a feeling that technologically, economically and politically the British had nothing to learn from India and much to teach. It did not take long for imperial arrogance to replace curiosity.

Religion played a major role too. Perhaps the most powerful of the new breed of hard-line critics of Indian culture was one of the Company's directors, Charles Grant. Grant was among the first of the new Evangelical Christians, and he brought his fundamentalist religious opinions directly to the East India Company Boardroom. Writing that "it is hardly possible to conceive any people more completely enchained than they [the Hindus] are by 'their superstitions," he proposed in 1787 to launch missions to convert a people whom he characterized "universally and wholly corrupt ... depraved as they are blind, and wretched as they are depraved." Within a few years, the missionaries – initially based at the Dutch settlement of Serampore – were beginning to fundamentally change British perceptions of the Hindus. No longer were they inheritors of a body of sublime and ancient wisdom as Jones and Hastings believed, but instead merely "poor benighted heathen," or even "licentious pagans," some of whom, it was hoped, were eagerly awaiting conversion, and with it the path to Civilization.

It was at this period too that you got the development for the first time of ideas of racial purity, of colour and ethnic hierarchy, and the beginnings of straightforward racialism: ideas which would of course reach their most horrifying denouement in the middle years of the twentieth century, but whose roots can be traced to developments in European thought a century earlier, and at least partly to developments in British India.

These new racial attitudes affected all aspects of relations between the British and Indians. The eighteenth and early nineteenth century had produced many "White Mughals" – characters like the British Resident at the Mughal court, Sir David Ochterlony. When in the Indian capital, Ochterlony liked to be addressed by his full Mughal title, Nasir-ud-Daula (Defender of the State) and to live the life of a Mughal gentleman: every evening all thirteen of Ochterlony's consorts used to process around Delhi behind their husband, each on the back of her own elephant. With his fondness for hookahs and nautch girls and Indian costumes, Ochterlony amazed Bishop Reginald Heber, the Anglican Primate of Calcutta, by receiving him sitting on a divan wearing a "choga and pagri" while being fanned by servants holding peacock feather punkhas.

Such people were becoming few and far between by the 1830's, and their way of life was beginning to die out. The Bengal Wills show that it was at this time that the number of Indian wives or Bibis being mentioned in wills and inventories begins to decline: from turning up in one in three wills from 1780 to 1785, the practice went into steep decline. Between 1805-10, Bibis appear in only one in every four wills; by 1830 it is one in six; by the middle of the century they have all but disappeared.

Englishmen who had taken on Indian customs likewise began to be objects of surprise even, on occasions, of derision in Calcutta. In the early years of the nineteenth century there was growing "ridicule" of men "who allow whiskers to grow and who wear turbans &c in imitation of the Mussulmans." Curries were no longer acceptable dishes for parties, and pyjamas – common dress in eighteenth century Calcutta and Madras – for the first time became something that an Englishman slept in rather than something he wore during the day. By 1813, Thomas Williamson was writing in *The European in India* how "The hookah, or pipe ... was very nearly universally retained among Europeans. Time, however, has retrenched this luxury so much, that not one in three now smokes." Soon the hookah was to go the way of the Bibi: into extinction.

Fanny stood in the middle of this process of change – this slow alienation of the British from the India they ruled – and was one of the last of the generation who was able to express unequivocal admiration for India, though even at the time her attitudes were clearly subject to criticism. On her travels, she found that Victorian religiosity was already beginning to make itself felt, and that attitudes were changing: "Methodism is gaining ground very fast in Cawnpore," she records. "Young ladies sometimes profess to believe it is highly incorrect to go to balls, plays, races, or to any party where it is possible there may be a quadrille. A number of the officers also profess these opinions, and set themselves up as new lights." In Calcutta she finds many of her contemporaries were "determined to be critical" of anything in India. When she visits an old Princess who was a cousin of the Gardners in the zenana of the Red Fort in Delhi, British opposition to Fanny's sympathies comes out into the open and she lets slip that that she was clearly regarded as suspect by the British in Delhi for mixing with (or even taking an interest in) the sad, impoverished descendants of the Great Mughals and fires back at the criticism, both of her and her Mughal hosts:

I heard that I was much blamed for visiting the princess, it being supposed that I went there for the sake of presents ... I went there for curiosity, not avarice ... Look at the poverty, the wretched poverty of these descendants of the Emperors! In former times strings of pearls and valuable jewels were placed on the necks of departing visitors. When the Princess Hyat-ool-Nissa Begum in her fallen fortunes put the necklace of freshly gathered white jasmine flowers over my head, I bowed with as much respect as if she had been the Queen of the Universe. Others may look upon these people with contempt, I cannot. Look at what they are what they have been.

One day a gentleman, speaking to me of the *extravagance* of one of the young princes, mentioned that he was always in debt, he could never live upon his allowance. The allowance of the prince was twelve rupees a month! Not more than the wages of a head servant.

With respect to my visit, I felt it hard to be judged by people who were ignorant of the fact of my being the friend of the relatives of those I visited in the zenana. People who themselves had, perhaps, no curiosity respecting native life and manners, and who, even if they had the curiosity, might have been utterly unable to gratify it, unless by an introduction they were probably unable to obtain.

With such criticism buzzing around her, it is hardly surprising therefore that Fanny took refuge and found friendship among an older generation of Indianized Europeans, men who had to some extent crossed cultures, just as she was beginning to do.

In Calcutta, she immediately fell for the dashing French General Allard, a Sergeant Major of Joseph Bonaparte's bodyguard, who left St Tropez and ended up commanding two regiments of dragoons and lancers for the Sikh leader Ranjit Singh in the Punjab, marrying a beautiful Kashmiri girl and more or less becoming a Sikh himself: "he is the most picturesque person imaginable," wrote Fanny after meeting him.

> His long forked beard, divided in the centre, hangs down on either side of his face; at dinner time he passes one end of his beard over one ear, and the other end over the other ear. I was much delighted with the General: he asked me to visit him in Lahore, an invitation I told him I would accept with great pleasure, should I ever visit the hills, and he told me he would send an escort for me.

Fanny forged a deeper relationship still with William Linnaeus Gardner, perhaps the single most intriguing character in Fanny's entire book. Gardner was born into a prominent American loyalist family on the banks of the Hudson. He had fled America after the Patriot victory in the War of Independence and finished his education in France and Holland, before sailing to India to make his fortune. There he inherited his father's peerage, married a beautiful Mughal Princess of Cambay and having fought for many years as a mercenary under a variety of Indian rulers he eventually resumed his allegiance to the British Crown and formed his own irregular regiment, Gardner's Horse.

Gardner was very much a family man, and in his private correspondence [now in the India Office Library] he talks proudly in his letters of his multi racial family: "Man must have a companion," he wrote to his cousin,

> And the older I get the more I am confirmed in this. An old age without something to love, and nourish and nurse you, must be cold and uncomfortable. The Begum and I, from 22 years' constant contact, have smoothed off each other's asperities and roll on peaceably and contentedly. Now I hope

both my boys will get me lots of grandchildren, for I find the grandpapa is the greatest favourite they have. The shouts of joy when I return after an absence of any time can be heard for a mile. My house is filled with Brats, and the very thinking of them, from blue eyes and fair hair to ebony and wool makes me quite anxious to get back again ... There's no accounting for taste but I have more relish in playing with the little brats than for the First Society in the World ... New books, a garden, a spade, nobody to obey, pyjamas, grandchildren, tranquillity: this is the summit of happiness, not only in the East but the West too.

Gardner's son James continued the family tradition by marrying Mukhta Begum who was the niece of the Mughal Emperor Akbar Shah as well as being the sister-in-law of the Nawab of Avadh, and together they fathered an Anglo-Mughal dynasty, half of whose members were Muslim and half Christian; indeed some of them such as James Jehangir Shikoh Gardner seem to have been both at the same time. Indeed even those Gardners who were straightforwardly Christian had alternative Muslim names: thus the Reverend Bartholomew Gardner could also be addressed as Sabr, under which name he was a notable Urdu and Persian poet, shedding his clerical dress in favour of Avadhi pyjamas to declaim his achingly beautiful love poems at Lucknavi mushairas.

Fanny's description of her visit to Gardner's jagir [or Mughal landed estate] at Khasgunge, her detailed exposition of how an English nobleman lived in a culturally hybrid house with a Mughal zenana, Mughal customs, and her account of Gardner's strange Anglo-Mughal wedding celebrations is the most fascinating section of her travel book, a unique record of an attractively multicultural world that was soon to vanish. Indeed Fanny was clearly a little in love with the dashing Colonel:

He must have been, and is, very handsome; such a high caste man! How he came to marry his Begum I know not. What a romance his love must have been! I wish I had his portrait, just as he now appears, so dignified and interesting. His partiality flatters me greatly!

It is also interesting that even at this stage that Gardner, though clearly a survivor – even a museum piece from a previous age – was nevertheless not alone in his tastes and sympathies. At the wedding of the Colonel's granddaughter, Fanny describes how the European guests, like their host, were all in Mughal dress. Later, "two English gentlemen, who were fond of native life, and fascinated with Khasgunge, requested me to mention to Colonel Gardner their wish to become of his family; I did so." It was the last gasp maybe, but the old inter-cultural hybridity was not yet completely finished.

William Gardner died on his Khasgunge estate on the 29th of July 1835, at the age of sixty five. His Begum, whose dark eyes he had first glimpsed through the chik in Surat thirty eight years earlier, could not live without him. Fanny's account of the death of Gardner's Begum is one of the most moving sections in the book:

> My beloved friend Colonel Gardner ... was buried, according to his desire, near the [domed Mughal] tomb of his son Allan. From the time of his death the poor Begum pined and sank daily; just as he said she complained not, but she took his death to heart; she died one month and two days after his decease. Native ladies have a number of titles; her death, names and titles were thus announced in the papers:– "On the 31st August, at her Residence at Khasgunge. Her Highness Furzund Azeza Azubdeh-tool Arrakeen Umdehtool Assateen Nuwab Mah Munzil ool Nissa Begum Dehlmi, relict of the late Colonel William Linnaeus Gardner. The sound of

55

Nakaras and *Dumanas* [kettle drums and trumpets] have ceased."

The following year Fanny returned, broken hearted and paid her respects at the grave of her beloved friend: "I knelt at the grave of my kind, kind friend and wept and prayed in deep affliction."

The family never really recovered the position they held under William. Despite possessing a pukka peerage, the Barony of Uttoxeter, over time, the family squandered their wealth and became poorer and poorer and more and more provincial Indian, gradually loosing touch with their aristocratic English relations. The penultimate Vicereign, Lady Halifax, had Gardner blood and records in her memoirs that she was a little surprised when alighting from the Viceregal train from Delhi on her way up to Simla, to see the Station Master of Kalka break through the ceremonial guard and fight his way up to the red carpet. Shouldering his way through the ranks of aides and the viceregal retinue, he addressed Her Excellency the Vicereine:

"Your Excellency," he said, "my name is Gardner."

"Of course," replied Lady Halifax, somewhat to the astonishment of the viceregal entourage. "We are therefore cousins."

The Gardner dynasty, incidentally still survives near Lucknow, today one of the most violent and backward parts of India. The present Lord Gardner who has never been to England and speaks only faltering English, contents himself with farming his Indian acres and enjoying the prestige of being the village wrestling champion, but who, until he recently missed his chance, threatened every so often to return "home" and take up his seat in the House of Lords.

Fanny enjoyed travel books, and mentions those of several of her male contemporaries in her text. She was well aware that her femininity made her vulnerable and so deprived her of opportunities open to them; but she also knew that she had one distinct advantage where she could trump her male rivals: her access to Indian zenanas. No Englishman could go into the quarters of Indian women, and Fanny was determined to make the most of the opportunity and to report from beyond a frontier that her rivals could not cross.

In Calcutta, in Lucknow, at Khasgunge and in Delhi Fanny repeatedly visits the women of different harems and reports about the life, the pleasures and the sorrows of the women she encounters there. One woman in particular she befriends, Baiza Bai, the dowager Maratha queen of Gwalior who had been deposed by her son and sent into exile at Fatighar in British territory not far from Cawnpore. Far from fantasizing the sensual pleasures to be had in the Eastern harem, as was the want of many of the male painters and writers of her time, Fanny reports on her perceptions of the reality of the lives of Indian women, and especially the restrictions which she felt women in both East and West suffered in common: "We spoke of the severity of the laws of England with respect to married women, how completely by law they are the slaves of their husbands, and how little hope there is of redress."

She also found a common love of riding with the Queen and describes learning to ride Maratha style, while trying to teach Baiza Bai's women how to ride sidesaddle. Always impatient with Western notions of feminine decorum Fanny records how "I thought of Queen Elizabeth, and her stupidity in changing the style of riding for women."

If Fanny was able to break some contemporary stereotypes about the life led by the inhabitants of Indian zenanas, she was less perceptive with her passages on Thuggee: the strangling and robbery of travellers by what the British came to believe was an India-wide brotherhood of Kali worshippers. Fanny devotes a great deal of space to the sensational reports then being circulated in the British press about the prevalence of thugs who were said to take the lives of literally tens of thousands of travellers every year. Today few would dispute that merchants and pilgrim bands were indeed very vulnerable to attack and robbery during this period; but most modern historians now believe that the British officials put in charge of the "Suppression of Thuggee" hugely exaggerated the scale of the problem and created a mythical All-India Thug Conspiracy where in reality there were only scattered groups of robbers and highwaymen. Some historians also allege that the British used the suppression of thuggee as an excuse and a justification for widening their area of rule: it was no coincidence that James Sleeman, the man who led the British campaign against the thugs, was also the man who wrote most vocally for the annexation of the Kingdom of Avadh.

Yet even here, while clearly fascinated by the threat and spectacle of thugee, and excited by the idea of a conspiracy of sacred stranglers, Fanny sounds a note of caution, remarking on hearing about the mass execution of a group of twenty five thugs that, "it cannot but be lamented that the course of justice is so slow; as these men, who were this day executed, have been in prison more than eight years for want of sufficient evidence." So saying, she leaves a question hanging in the air. If the thugs were so guilty, how come there was so little evidence? It was certainly an apposite query. In normal circumstances, courts in India did not accept the statements of approvers who turned "King's Evidence"; but in the case of thugs colonial laws were altered to allow the conviction of thugs on evidence which would in other circumstances be regarded as suspect and inadequate.

The same Evangelical Victorian colonial attitudes that wished to sell the Taj Mahal for marble and demolish the monuments of Agra was also the world that dreamed up India-wide thug conspiracies. It was not a world where Indian and English could cohabit on any terms of equality, and Fanny Parkes was one of the last English writers to believe – or even to want to believe – that mutually respectful relationships were possible or even desirable. The inevitable clash came in the Indian Mutiny of 1857, when the East India Company's own troops rose in rebellion, joined in much of North India by great swathes of the civilian population. Nowhere was this more the case than in the supposedly "degenerate" and "effeminate" towns of Mughal Delhi and Lucknow where the British only defeated the rebels with the very greatest difficulty and with unimaginable causalities on both sides.

The world beloved of William Gardner and General Allard, and indeed of Fanny herself, was swept away in the mutiny. The uprising led to massive bloodshed, desperate atrocities and with great numbers of lives lost on either side. During the fighting, Gardner's Anglo-Indian descendants, like those of all the other White Mughals, were forced to make a final choice between one or other of the two sides – though for many the choice was made for them. After an attack on their property, the Gardners were forced to take refuge first in Aligarh then in the Fort of Agra, and so also ended up on the side of the British – though given a free hand they might just as easily have lined up behind their Mughal cousins in Delhi and Lucknow.

Afterwards, nothing could ever be as it was. With the British victory, and the genocidal spate of hangings and executions that followed, the entire top rank of the Mughal aristocracy was swept away and British culture was unapologetically imposed on India; at the same time the wholesale arrival of the memsahibs ended all open sexual contact between the two nations. White Mughals like Ochterlony and Gardner died out, and their very existence was later delicately erased from embarrassed Victorian history books. Only now is their existence beginning to be unearthed. Moreover at a time when respectable journalists and academics are again talking of the Clash of Civilizations, and when East and West, Islam and Christianity are again engaged in a major confrontation, Fanny's record of this hybrid world has never been more important.

At the time of her travels, Fanny Parkes was criticized by her contemporaries for "Going Native," for her over-developed sympathies for cultures, religions and peoples of North India. Today she is under assault from the opposite direction.

Following the success of Edward Said's groundbreaking work *Orientalism* there has developed a whole school of criticism which has attempted to apply Said's ideas to the whole range of colonial writings and art. Some of these applications have proved more suitable than others, and there sometimes seems to be an assumption at work in academia – especially in the US – that all writings of the colonial period exhibit exactly the same set of prejudices: a monolithic modern academic Occidentalism which seems uncannily to match the monolithic stereotypes of the original Orientalism.

Fanny has not escaped this academic pigeon-holing, and has recently been the subject of two academic articles which would have her implicit in the project of gathering "Colonial knowledge" and "imbricated with the project of Orientalism" – in other words an unwitting outrider of colonialism, attempting to "appropriate" Indian learning and demonstrate the superiority of Western ways by "imagining" India as decayed and degenerate, fit only to be colonized and "civilized." Anyone who reads Fanny's writing with an open mind cannot but see this as a wilful misreading of her text, an attempt to fit her book into a mould which it simply does not fit. There are many writers of the period to which such strictures could be applied, but it seems misguided in the extreme to see Parkes as any sort of gung-ho colonialist. Fanny was a passionate lover of India and though a woman of her time, in her writing and her travels did her best to understand and build bridges across the colonial divide.

As Colin Thubron has pointed out,

> [T]ravel itself is traditionally subversive. The vagabond, the gypsy, and the expatriate: they are those without allegiance ... To define the genre [of travel writing] as an act of domination — rather than of understanding, respect or even catharsis — is simplistic. If even the attempt to understand is seen as aggression or appropriation, then all human contact declines into paranoia.

The point is well made, and the attacks made on Fanny by modern academic critics highlights the problem with so much of that has been written about eighteenth and early nineteenth century India: the temptation felt by so many critics to project onto it the stereotypes of Victorian and Edwardian behaviour and attitudes with which we are so familiar.

Yet these attitudes were clearly entirely at odds with the actual fears and hopes, anxieties and aspirations of many of the eighteenth and early nineteenth century Company officials and their Indian wives whose writings can be read with the greatest of ease in books such as Fanny's *Wanderings,* quite apart from the fifty miles of East India Company documents and letters stored in the India Office Library in London. It is as if Victorians succeeded in colonizing not just India but also, more permanently, our imaginations, to the exclusion of all other images of the Indo-British encounter.

The travel book, by its very nature, records the transitory moment: as Thubron puts it, a good travel book "catches the moment on the wing, and stops it in Time." Fanny Parkes' wonderful book is an important historical text for its record of the last moments of this very attractive (and largely forgotten) moment of cultural and sexual interaction and crossover: what Salman Rushdie — talking of modern multiculturalism – has called "chutnification." The world described by Fanny – especially the syncretic culture of Lucknow and Delhi, and its satellite at Khasgunge – was far more hybrid, and had far less clearly defined ethnic, national and religious borders than we have been conditioned to expect, either by the conventional Imperial history books written in Britain before 1947, or by the nationalist historiography of post-Independence India. It was a world where British mercenaries married Mughal princesses and where Anglo-Indian women entered the harems of Nawabi Avadh, where Muslims attended Hindu ceremonies and vice versa.

This account of Fanny Parkes' writing represents my own personal selection of her work, but I hope it at least conveys a flavour of her writing and reveals a little of the largely forgotten world she so loved and enjoyed.

COLONIALISM, SURVEILLANCE AND MEMOIRS OF TRAVEL: TEGART'S DIARIES AND THE ANDAMAN CELLULAR JAIL

TUTUN MUKHERJEE

How do people get to this clandestine Archipelago? Hour by hour planes fly there, ships steer their course there, and trains thunder off to it — but all with nary a mark on them to tell of their destination.[1]

In the last few decades, matters of empire and colony have assumed great significance in the understanding and interpretation of literature and culture. It is not surprising that this should be so. Though the era of high nineteenth-century imperialism ended after the Second World War, the reality of the imperial past and of the historical experience of colonialism remain vivid as the shared memory of the ruler and the ruled, and colour their expression and perception of culture, ideology and politics.

The appeal to the colonial past to interpret the postcolonial present is not just an expedient strategy. It constitutes a revisionist inquiry into the enterprise of the empire that created structures and institutions to perpetuate colonialism and tried to incorporate within its disciplinary discourses, the land, the culture, and the history of the colony. It also throws light upon the postcolonial predicament or the inheritance of the politics of difference that was deeply interwoven with practices of colonial control. That the basis of social life remains deeply infected by ideas of difference and division even in the absence of foreign rule, is a sobering postcolonial realization.

By its very definition, empire denotes the effective control of one state over the political sovereignty of another society or state, achieved by force, political collaboration, or by economic, social or cultural domination. Yet, neither imperialism nor colonialism is a simple act of expansion and acquisition. Albeit urged by capitalist economies, the final claim over territories and possessions, geography and power is often supported by ideological aspirations. So, besides the desire for economic gain and political power, the colonial consciousness prioritizes certain cultural motivations.[2] Hence, the empire's ethnocentric zeal to "educate" and "civilize" the "natives" is ensured approval of the metropolis for the political technologies of colonialism that includes the penetration of its ideological machinery into the so-called primitive/savage cultures.[3] One is aware of the impressive range of historical studies on the impact of European ideologies on the Third World countries, and the fashioning by the West of the categories of difference and the backwardness to describe the people of the non-West – thus essentialized and othered, producing what is now termed as alterity – and justify the domination of the West. This also justifies the enforcing and maintaining of the new hierarchies in the social body.[4]

Yet, it cannot be ignored that the ideological thrust of the Empire that encouraged the flow of liberal ideas and social norms from the West into the colonies also quickened the spirit of nationalism in the colonized peoples. In turn, this soon channelled into forms of native resistance.

Any institution based on force and domination can survive only as long as it is able to overcome the resistance of individuals or groups by force. When it is compelled to use force repeatedly, it has conceded to having provoked serious revolutionary situations, challenging its organs of authority. The culture of colonialism presumes a particular style of managing dissent. The survival of colonialism depends on its abilities to promptly arrest insurgent activities. Empires are established and maintained not merely by military superiority, or by clever manipulation/exploitation of the colony's divisive social tensions [there is evidence of tremendously risky physical disparity between the small number of colonizers at a very great distance from home, and the much larger number of natives on their home territory],[5] but because they deploy a sophisticated intelligence and surveillance system for the identification and containment of rebellious elements. The quality of military and political intelligence available to the colonial power very often proves to be the critical determinant of its success in conquest and profitable governance. This is the body of information that the masters frequently draw upon and depend upon to understand the political and economic activities and cultures of their colonies and their indigenous subjects. Surveillance and intelligence networks then form the core of imperial governance, empowering it with critical knowledge of the strategies to pre-empt revolutions/insurgence, and with the technologies of discipline and punishment.

Webster's Dictionary defines "surveillance" as "a close watch kept over a suspect group or a person and implies in public mind that the behaviour of the 'surveilled' is not legitimate political behaviour. The application of surveillance stigmatizes, that is, it labels as deviant and illegitimate the behaviour of those involved." The efficacy of the surveillance system determines the power spectrum of colonial masters. As Foucault says, "Power is not a commodity, a position, a prize or a plot; it is the operation of the political technologies throughout the social body ... The functioning of these rituals of power is exactly what sets up the non-egalitarian asymmetrical relationships."[6] It is possible to unveil the nexus of power by isolating, identifying and analyzing the web of unequal relationships. It is important to understand how power operates.

II

Colonial settlement has invariably been expressed textually.[7] Vast textual archives give evidence of the Empire being conceived and maintained in an array of writings: political treatises, acts and edicts, administrative records and gazettes, government briefs, the colonial offices' reports, notebooks, diaries, memoirs, missionaries' reports, travel writing and letters "home." In this segment of the paper, I examine a text that makes accessible to analysis the enterprise of the Empire in India and its political network that ensured the Empire's continued power over the colonial subject. Rather than as a récit de voyage, I would like to study the text as a discourse de voyage in order to affiliate the chronotope of travel to the strategies of domination in the discourse of imperialism.

Charles Augustus Tegart, son of an Irish clergyman, Reverend J P Tegart, was a British loyalist who came to India as Inspector of Police, Intelligence Branch, in 1901. His first post was Pataliputra, which then came within the larger province of Bengal. He came to Calcutta in 1906 as Deputy Commissioner of Police. He was elevated to the post of Police Commissioner in 1923, and remained in India till 1931. He went to England for a vacation (and also to have his appendix removed) in 1931. He was offered a job in the Council of the Secretary of State for India at London, and so resigned his job in India. In 1933, Trinity College honoured him with the degree of LLD (Doctor of Law). In 1936, King George VI bestowed the KCIE (Knight Commander of the Order of the Indian Empire) upon him. In 1946, he suffered several cardiac attacks and died soon after. His wife, Kathleen, wrote a three hundred forty page manuscript called *Memoir of an Indian Policeman*, in which she compiled

Tegart's Diaries and file reports and wove them together with her own story about two Bengali revolutionaries called Naren and Biren.[8]

The *Memoir* records a particularly violent chapter in the history of colonial India – the British encounter with armed struggle and extremism. Anglo-Indian history generally interprets the dramatic onset of the Revolt of 1857 as an acute failure in British intelligence – gathering and analysis – in direct contrast to, as Sir John Kaye notes, the "almost electric" manner in which the rebels and the Indian population disseminated information about the British activities, weaknesses and disasters.[9] In the post-Mutiny context, the Empire not only concentrated on establishing a more professional police network, but also on the containment and continued surveillance of the seditious elements. The shift in British attitudes after the 1857 Sipahi Revolt was palpable and no efforts were spared to make the political surveillance and military intelligence more effective. Historians have argued that in the post-1857 years the Raj became a kind of police state.[10] Correspondingly, the indigenous reaction became increasingly violent. Curzon's provocative actions had already fired nationalist passions, and the Minto-Morley repressive measures did nothing to quell them. There was renewed attraction for the methods of revolutionary terrorism, especially among sections of educated youth in the regions of Bengal, Uttar Pradesh and Punjab. The targets of attack by bomb or gunshot were important officials, police and bureaucratic personnel, British loyalists and informers. As revolutionary attacks became frequent, Tilak's call for mass action had a resounding response. Interestingly, his exhortation emphasised the control of the information network. He said: "... [T]hough downtrodden and neglected, you must be conscious of your power of making administration impossible if you choose to make it so. It is you who manage the railroad and the telegraph, it is you who make settlements and collect revenues ..."[11] The tendency toward individual aggressiveness became more pronounced.

India witnessed the most intense phase of revolutionary and terrorist actions between 1900 and 1931. It seems a strange coincidence that this period exactly parallels Tegart's stay in India. Indeed, Tegart's diaries and file reports indicate a causal relationship with the young revolutionaries of Bengal. He hunted them and was hunted himself. He escaped several attacks miraculously – either by the grace of god or by the grace of the intelligence network! Tegart remained ever vigilant. As the *Memoir* describes,

> ... [Tegart] had a life-size sketch of a Bengali assassin, levelling a pistol, made on canvas which was kept on the roof and when another officer (usually Mr Colson who afterwards succeeded him as Commissioner) joined in the practice, it was the custom for one or the other of them, while they did the morning exercise to give a sudden unpremeditated yell; on this the other had to switch around with his automatic and shoot the canvas gunman in some vital part of his anatomy ...[12]

Other than direct encounter deaths, the Empire devised another method to arrest and disperse the revolutionary social energy. Besides the Rowlatt Act, a special police ordinance was passed to allow surveillance over all kinds of activities. The slightest hint of sedition led to immediate apprehension and imprisonment. The political prisoners or the detainees were often denied the benefit of a fair trial; an informer's report was enough to incriminate them.[13] Capital punishment was common enough for the revolutionaries till the British Empire thought of the idea of transportation for life. This was in keeping with the changes in the concept of discipline and punishment that had taken place in Europe. According to Foucault, the Western systems of administering justice and the concept of punishment changed radically through the eighteenth and nineteenth centuries with the growing awareness of the forces of productive capital. Instead of revenge through torture chambers and slaughterhouses, the aim of the punishment process came to be seen as either correction or containment for the preservation of a social order. The centre of this new process is what Foucault calls discipline that has to be measured and continuous, though not spectacular. A technology of observation is essential to it. Foucault discusses the Benthamite Panopticon as a model for the perfectly efficient mechanism of surveillance, a technical structure that ensures the unrelieved presence of the watcher for the watched. The convict in the Panopticon is "seen, but he does not see; he may be the object of information but never a subject in communication."[14]

During their occupation of India, the British built on the Andaman Islands one such instance of control and punishment, a nexus of power for the containment and dispersal of revolutionary social energy – the dreaded Cellular Jail, a Gulag Archipelago into which all dissent and non-conformity could be funnelled.

On the map, the Andaman and Nicobar Islands seems a small lush green cluster where the Bay of Bengal opens into the Indian Ocean. It was rediscovered by the Western World (Marco Polo touched the Islands in the fifteenth century on his way back from China) by the surveyors and travellers of the East India Company and the British Empire. Captains John Ritchie in 1777, and Thomas Forrest and Hamilton Buchanan in 1783 surveyed the Islands as a possible site for the East India Company, a site that could cater to ships in distress in the vast expanse of the Indian Ocean, especially during the monsoons, and also to control the Malay pirates. Later, Lieutenant Archibald Blair mapped the Islands, and his report on their strategic importance as well as their out-of-reachness made the Andamans the obvious choice for the penal colony along with the armed outpost that the British planned to build after the 1857 uprising. On 15 January 1858, the Governor General in the Council considered it tactical to "colonize" the Islands, and resolved "to establish a penal settlement on the Andamans for the reception in the first instance of convicts sentenced to imprisonment or to transportation, for crimes of mutiny and rebellion and for other offences therewith ..."[15] This method of segregation of the people to discipline and control was a new feature of the British administration. The construction of the jail was completed in 1908, and thereafter it became the jail for life prisoners. Mostly political prisoners and those sentenced to die were condemned to the prison of the Andamans. Some of the most daring leaders of the Indian freedom struggle were sent there. Because exile for life seemed to most people like living death, the deportation to the Islands came to be called "Kala Pani" or the final journey to the place of permanent exile, the legendary hell from which no one ever returned. Indeed, in the span of twenty years, which constituted the period of imprisonment, the convict would lose all links not only with his family but also with civilization. "Kala pani," literally meaning "black water," referring to the taboo of crossing the seas, gradually acquired an aura of uncanny fear about it. Even those who could survive the incarceration were exposed to a synonymous danger of black-water fever, a virulent form of malaria.

In 1880, Radhacharan Goswami, an ardent member of the Indian National Congress, serialized in the *Sarasudhanidhi*, a prominent Hindi periodical, a narrative called "Yamalok ki Yatra." It described the visit of an "enlightened" young man to the kingdom of Yama, the god of death. This was a special hell created for those who had fought the British in 1857. The correspondence was intentional. Such images were replicated in many write-ups, as for example, in Colonel Wedgewood's description of "Hell on Earth" (1921) and in Bijoy Kumar Sinha's *Andaman: The Indian Bastille* (1939). Clearly, the Andaman Cellular Jail is vested with great sentimental significance for the Indian people.

In 1913, Charles Tegart travelled to the Andamans on a special mission. Not satisfied with the way the confrontation with the Bengal revolutionaries was going, he wanted to extract all information about such activities from the inmates of the jail who had been implicated in various cases of bombing and sedition. He was empowered by his Government to suspend the sentences of those who divulged information that would prove helpful to the Government. Tegart sailed for Rangoon on Sunday, 24th August 1913 by the *BISS Arankola*. Travelling with him were the famous revolutionary Nonigopal Mukhopadhyay's brother, Surendra Mukherjee, and the lawyer Raisaheb S K Mahapatra. The plan was to use not only political but also emotional and psychological inducement to elicit information from the prisoners. Tegart reached Rangoon on 26th August, and started his trip to the Andamans by *SS Maharaja*. In his Diary, he notes that they travelled through the monsoons and reached the verdant islands after two days. Charmed by the beauty and the isolation of the place, he rationalizes the existence of a penal institution in such a place.

The idea of a penal colony was already a part of the colonial technology. As Foucault emphasises, the systems of punishment in contemporary societies are situated in a certain political economy of the body. It is always the body that is in issue – the body and its forces, its utility, and its docility, its distribution and submission. The body is directly involved in a political field; power relations have an immediate hold upon it; they invest it, mark it, train it, torture it, force it to carry out tasks, to perform ceremonies, to emit signs. This political investment of the body is bound up in accordance with complex reciprocal relations, with its economic use; it is largely as a force of production that the body is invested with relations of power and domination. But the constitution of labour power is possible only if it is caught up in a system of discipline and subjection. Discipline, as Foucault describes it, emerges as a structuring in space and time of the activity of work. Discipline seeks also to mould "souls" through the body; the disciplined subject is one whose actions and reactions are totally under control. This

71

subject is, finally, a subject of knowledge through systematic examination and surveillance. And since this needs sets of norms against which individuals may be measured, a political instrument has to be meticulously prepared and used. This subjection can be obtained by instruments of violence or ideology; it can also be direct and physical, pitting force against force. Thus, the body is useful only as a productive body or a subjected one.

Illustrative of the effectiveness of such correctional discipline is the report on the convict system and progress in the Andaman Settlement submitted by the Chief Commissioner in Residence, Lieutenant Colonel R C Temple:

> ... The convict comes to the Andamans, a creature who by his life or his acts, has shown himself to be so unfitted for human society that he has been cast out of it for life, or for a long term of years. Received thus, he is first subjected for six months to a most severe discipline – hard, rigid, uncompromising. He is taught what it is like to be forced to bend his uncontrolled nature to the iron yoke of a regime ... he is next transferred to work in the company with others, but still under a strict discipline ... Here he stays for a year and a half, and then for the next three years he is a slave, as the word is ordinarily understood, locked up with other slaves in the barracks at night, but well-fed, housed, clothed, and cared for and always under watch and guard. During the following five years he is still a labouring convict, but the severity of his life is eased down a little ... having thus served ten long probationary years he is eligible, if he has any capacity to take a ticket-of-leave and become what is locally known as a self-supporter. The convict is now in a sense "free" ... It does not require much imagination to contrast the difference in the personality of the same human being as he reaches and leaves Port Blair. He that arrived an outcast,

void of restraint, and unfit for association with his kind on equal terms, goes forth a useful citizen, broken to restraint, and not only fitted for human society, but well used to submit to the conventions by which alone that society can be maintained ... the incorrigibles are kept till death, and the slow to learn are kept until they mend their ways ...[16]

In effect, discipline is the technique by which the body is reduced as a "political" force and maximized as a useful force.

According to Tegart, the administration would not have recommended such methods had there been any alternatives and had the administration not been satisfied with the effectiveness of the prison system in the Andaman Cellular Jail. Tegart's Diaries describe the technology of the penal architecture that ensures continuous surveillance of the political criminals who are more dangerous because they violate the law motivated by the desire to influence existing policy and power relations. Their goals are not personal gains, but broader social contexts. Sentences passed on them are necessarily harsh. Transportation for life for the political prisoner meant a life of oblivion.

No one could remain immune to the beauty of the Islands. For example, V D Savarkar was enchanted by his first glimpse of the Islands, and writes: "The Island ornamented the sea like a palace built in the land of the fairies ... It was so picturesque and compact that it could not fail to ravish the mind of even a prisoner in chains like me."[17]

Tegart comments on the appropriateness of the disciplinary structure — so stark in an environment of beauty — intended for visual and auditory deprivation, and physical curtailment of freedom for those fighting for freedom. Tegart describes the circle of well-lit cells facing inwards with the surveillance tower as the hub. The entire set-up was intended to dissociate power from the people, investing it in topological configuration of light, bodies, gaze and

73

architecture – and thus becoming automatic, residing in the arrangement itself. Hemmed by obdurate structures, locked doors, guards on duty, barbed wire, gun tower, electric cable, the prison was structured for total control and deprivation of the prisoners of auditory and visual information. It would seem that with imprisonment in the Andamans, life stopped ... but only apparently so. Tegart's account suggests his dissatisfaction with the rule of letting the prisoners roam about freely within the Settlement. He notes that besides the incidents of prisoners escaping, there existed a surreptitious but regular supply of seditious material to the prisoners. Moreover, those incarcerated within the four walls made their bodies the site of resistance. Tegart records that Nonigopal, for example, was totally uncooperative and refused even to wear clothes. There were many who refused to talk or eat. Tegart travels through the island archipelago, and his alert eyes, indifferent to the tropical beauty, only sought evidence of lapse of vigilance that afforded the prisoners opportunities to mingle and conspire. Surveillance, according to him, was the awareness of the Other, and a constant vigil to pre-empt dangerous irruptions of any kind.

Tegart's Diary is fascinating not only because it retains traces of the violent history of colonial intervention, but also because it instantiates the case of travel for a specific purpose within the imperialist agenda.

III

For the purposes of the Empire's territorial aggrandizement and consolidation, colonialism was a metaphoric and cartographic as well as a legalistic enterprise. The occupied country was invariably "mapped" or spatially conceived.

In support of my discourse de voyage I would like to place two other records of travel in the Andamans alongside Tegart's text. One travel account is intended to assist the Empire's enterprise of colonization, and the other – the traveller's rough, rudimentary description "charting" unknown lands – is illustrative of the Orientalist-touristic fascination for the Other. The first record is that of Lieutenant Colonel Archibald Blair, whose survey of the Islands is full of information, judgements, evaluations, and opinions. He writes with the awareness of his report's relevance to the Imperial design. He records his findings thus:

> ... It is hardly possible to conceive a more secure and perfect harbour. It is large enough to contain about fifty sails ... perfectly sheltered from all winds and sea, and though there is seven feet rise of tide, there is no stream to incommode ships under repair. Its situation renders it easy of access in either Monsoon, and ships may quit it at all seasons, and here it is proper to observe that the harbours of this island are better situated ...[18]

On the subject of the aborigines, he writes:

> In the morning we ... had a visit from the natives; after some hesitation they came close under the stern; they accepted some knives and looking glasses, but seemed very indifferent about them. On showing them bottles they expressed a great desire for them ... They were peaceable but extremely suspicious ... Like those we have seen on Interview Island, they were perfectly naked, their features, colour and hair resembling those of the natives of Africa ...[19]

Blair's style of writing is analytical and detailed. He includes especially curious features of the landscape, as for example, the "birds' nest caves":

> ... The entrance, which is washed by the tide, is an irregular aperture, of about six feet wide, and the same height. On advancing thirty or forty feet, the height diminishes to twenty.

Here it is rather dark and very warm, and the top and sides of the cave are covered with nests; an astonishing number of birds twittering and on the wing, whisking past the ears and eyes. This, contrasting with the melancholy noise of the waves resounding through the gloomy cavern, formed a very uncommon and interesting scene ...[20]

The noteworthy feature about Blair's report is that the territories are described as virgin land and not as a place with human history. Often the effect of such descriptions is to erase, either wholly or in part, the signs of other lives that occupied that particular space. As Elleke Boehmer explains, wherever the colonizers established their settlements, "they proclaimed the start of a new history. Other histories by definition were declared to be of lesser significance or in certain situations, non existent."[21]

Significantly different from Tegart's and Blair's travel reports is C Boden Kloss's *Andamans and Nicobar: The Narrative of a Cruise in the Schooner "Terrapin."* While the first two "reports" convey *information*, Kloss's "narrative" conveys *experience*. The main purpose of the Terrapin crew is ethnographical search, or in other words, the penetration of the encrypted aborigine society to document native life and custom before it was touched by ideas of progress, and thereby supplement the existing knowledge about the "early" stages of human history. Kloss describes their arrival at Port Blair:

... The whole place – in itself of natural beauty – is kept in most perfect condition by a practically unlimited supply of convict labour.

At first sight, it seemed an altogether delightful spot to find in such an isolated corner of the earth; but its melancholy aspect is quickly and forcibly brought home by a visit to the jail and by the continuous presence of the convicts, who are rendered conspicuous by their fetters, or neck-rings, supporting the numbered badges by which the wearers are distinguished.[22]

Kloss's description of the natives of the Island is openly ethnocentric:

The first thought that flashed into one's mind on perceiving them, with their small stature, sooty skins, and frizzy hair, was that here were a number of juvenile negroes ("niggers"); they are, however, far better looking than that people, and some of the women might even be called pretty, even when judged from a European standpoint.[23]

As illustration of the civilizing mission that the Empire has been pursuing, Kloss describes the architecture of the Chief Commissioner's bungalow and the soldiers' barracks (built in the Windsor style), as well as the club houses, swimming pools, badminton, tennis and golf courses, and cricket grounds, built for the exclusive use of the European officers and their families, as examples of the Western civilizing influence already in place.

IV

Narrative is intimately connected with the production of knowledge and thus also to power and desire. Such descriptions as are cited from Tegart, Blair and Kloss are integral to travel narratives. Journeys are undertaken and travelogues are written. The texts as vehicles of imperial "authority" symbolize and in many cases perform the act of "taking possession." All travel accounts during the Raj are noteworthy for the way imperial enterprise is encoded in the narratives.

In their production of knowledge, in their strengthening of the Empire's territorial and economic claims, in the furthering of the ideological mission, all the three texts discussed above prove this point. For instance, all three of them carry a lot of landscape description of the exploratory kind, supportive of the nineteenth century expansionist strategies. There is much "development oriented" description of the colonies, perhaps as an attempt to focus upon the areas "opening up" before European eyes. There is also the way the Other is described – collectively, in an inventory of traits and customs – rather in the manner of a lesson in the anthropology of the Third World. Stereotypically, all the three narratives present the Orient as the site of hazard and adventure. It is in the light of this textuality of the empire that the theoretical term, colonialist discourse, may be best understood. The analysis of such a discourse reveals the symbolic practices, including textual codes and conventions and implied meanings, which are deployed to secure imperial designs and also to decode the apparently unintelligible strangeness that the colonizers encounter. Therefore, underlying the discourse of imperial mastery are other responses like wonder, bewilderment, fear, that necessitate the constitution of "systems of cognition" like European names, practices and architecture as comfortable interpretive screens.[24]

However, the three texts are not all of a kind. Clearly, they exemplify different kinds of authority at work. While for Kloss, subjectivity and perspectivism are the anchors of textual authority, for Tegart and Blair impersonal knowledge and professional preoccupations are the governing factors. While Tegart's is an in-depth report of a surveillance officer, for Blair, information is the object, to be carried back to the Empire, because that information has the power to shape the Empire's expansionist plans. Kloss's experiential narrative extends the ideology of the civilizing mission.

It must be acknowledged that colonialism need not simply begin with the establishment of alien rule and end with the departure of alien rulers from the colony. Colonialism also connotes a state of mind or social consciousness that often persists in the political and social practices of the postcolonial state. Invariably, the administrative grid of the postcolonial state perpetuates the colonial politics of difference – between the ruler and the ruled. So, modern societies continue to maintain the institutions of discipline and punishment – like the prison, the asylum, the hospital, and the school – and perpetuate the practice of societal segregation of the un/anti-social, the abnormal, the unhealthy, and the uninitiated. As the French fableist La Fontaine wrote in 1668, those who seek to remain in power always arrange matters so as to give their tyranny the appearance of justice. This view seems endorsed by Freud's *Civilization and Its Discontents* wherein Freud explains man's capabilities in devising systems of control and segregation because man's impulse to cruelty arises from his instinct for mastery. Indeed, as the present world order informs us, the nations of the postcolonial and postmodern world are burdened with greater policing and surveillance systems than ever before.[25]

But the Cellular Jail of Andamans was closed after India's Independence in 1947 to signify the end of colonial rule. The Jail became a historical landmark, "hallowed" by the visit of Netaji Subhas Bose on 29th December, 1943. The lives of the political prisoners incarcerated in these islands became immortalized in Indian hearts. In this timeless limbo were placed men like Sher Khan who killed Lord Mayo and went to the gallows valiantly after receiving the Qalma like a true Wahabi, the young freedom fighters who left their narratives of pain carved on the prison walls, and the government doctor Dewan Singh who became the informer for the Imperial Nippon Army and was later killed by the Japanese.[26] The Andaman Cellular Jail acquired metaphorical force as the Indian Bastille. Eventually it became established as a temple of freedom in Independent India.

New mappings of history generate new meanings and configurations of altered significance. Representations and emblems of history return as commodity. The Andamans and its

Cellular Jail continue to attract travellers – but of a different kind now. The island and the prison have undergone the inevitable commodification to be sold to tourists as relics of history, both anthropological and cultural. The Andamans is no longer a British colony; the Ardamanese, some of whom claim to be descendants of the "free convicts" of the Settlement, are citizens of the Indian Republic. Understandably, there is a penchant for highlighting the idyllic and the exotic atmosphere of the islands; but the historical dimension must never be forgotten. So that the metaphor for the past remains relevant in the present, it is hoped that in the postcolonial situation, life in the Andamans will mirror the spirit of freedom lest it be said that white imperialism was simply replaced by brown imperialism.

Notes

1   Aleksandr I Solzhenitsyn, *The Gulag Archipelago, 1918-1956 (Vols.I-IV)*, Translated by Thomas P Whitney, (New York and London: Harper Row Publishers, 1974), 3.

2   In the Introduction to a group of essays on *British Imperialism: Gold, God, Glory* (New York & London: Holt, Rhinehart, Winston, 1963), Robin W Wicks suggests as "a rational theory for irrational drives," three motivations for imperialism: a) man's greed and search for wealth when economic motivations dominate him; b) man's idealism to create a better world expressed through brave actions and exalted statements; c) man's quest for power, for personal and collective glory, by instincts both base and noble.

3   By degrees, the "public school spirit" became one of the most potent of imperial elixirs. It inculcated a loyalty devoted to the "White Man's Burden" rather than to any particular practice of Empire. Illustrative of such sentiments was the tremendous popularity of the works of John Buchan, G A Henty, Frank Richards, Rider Haggard, Terence Rattigan, Rudyard Kipling and the travelogues of the legendary David Livingstone. For insightful discussions on this subject, see Walter E Houghton, *The Victorian Frame of Mind* (New Haven: Yale University Press, 1959); L D Wurgaft, *The Imperial Imagination* (Middletown, Conn.: Wesleyan University Press, 1983); Patrick Brantlinger, *Rule of Darkness: British Literature and Imperialism: 1830-1914* (Cornell University Press, 1988);

Joseph Bristow, *Empire Boys: Adventures in a Man's World* (New York & London: Harper Collins,1991).

4   James Mill's *History of British India* (1820) had tremendous influence on imperialist thinking of the time and shaped its policies. His work marshalled what he believed to be the useful facts to show the necessity of British rule as a remedy for India's "traditional tyranny and chaos" and to reposition India as an object of "reform."

5   Thomas B Macauley has famously written, "Empire is itself the strangest of all political anomalies. That a handful of adventurers from an island in the Atlantic should have subjugated a vast country divided from the place of their birth by half the globe ... are prodigies to which the world has seen nothing similar." In G W Young, *Speeches*, (Oxford: Oxford University Press, 1935), 153.

6   Michel Foucault, *Discipline and Punish: The Birth of the Prison*, English translation by Alan Sheridan, (London and New York: Vintage, 1979), 24.

7   Ronald Hyam, *Britain's Imperial Century, 1815-1914*, (New York and London: Macmillan. 1993).

8   Among the young revolutionaries imprisoned for involvement in the 1913 Alipore bomb blast case were two famous brothers, Aurobindo Ghosh and Barindra Ghosh. This could have inspired the choice of names.

9   John W Kaye, *The Administration of the East India Company*, (London: Oxford University Press, 1853), 354-355.

10   David Arnold, *Police Power and Colonial Rule, Madras 1859-1947*, (New Delhi: Oxford University Press, 1986), 1-6.

11   As quoted in C A Bayley, *Empire and Intelligence*, (Cambridge: Cambridge University Press, 1996), 364.

12   Kathleen Tegart, [unpublished manuscript], *Memoir of an Indian Policeman* (containing entries from C A Tegart's Diaries), India Office Library, London, 184.

13   John W Kaye, *The Administration of the East India Company*, 354-355.

14   Foucault, *Discipline and Punish: The Birth of the Prison*, 25.

15   L P Mathur, *History of the Andaman and Nicobar Islands, 1756-1966*, (New Delhi: Sterling Publishers, 1968), 68.

16   Boden C Kloss, *Andamans and Nicobars: The Narrative of a Cruise in the Schooner "Terrapin,"* (New Delhi: Vivek Publishing House, 1971), 193-199.

17   V D Savarkar, *The Story of My Transportation for Life: A Biography of Black Days in Andamans*, Translated by V N Naik, (Bombay: Sadbhakti Publishers, 1950), 8.

18   As quoted in Iqbal N Singh, *The Andaman Story*, (New Delhi: Vikas Publishing House, 1978), 21-22.

19   Iqbal N Singh, *The Andaman Story*, 26-27.

20   Iqbal N Singh, *The Andaman Story*, 26-27.

2 1   Elleke Boehmer, *Colonial and Postcolonial Literature*, (Oxford and New York: Oxford University Press, 1995), 24.

2 2   Boden C Kloss, *Andamans and Nicobars: The Narrative of a Cruise in the Schooner "Terrapin,"* 20-21.

2 3   Boden C Kloss, *Andamans and Nicobars: The Narrative of a Cruise in the Schooner "Terrapin,"* 24.

2 4   Boden C Kloss, *Colonial and Postcolonial Literature*, 50.

2 5   Sigmund Freud, *Civilization and its Discontents*, Translated by James Strachey, (New York: Norton & Co., 1961), 8.

2 6   The Japanese imperial design made a mockery of handing over these islands to the INA. After suffering severe setbacks in the Second World War, on 13th August 1945, two days before their surrender, the Japanese gunned down 300 villagers at Tarmugu.

References

1   Arnold, David, *Police Power and Colonial Rule, Madras 1859-1947*, (New Delhi: Oxford University Press, 1986).

2   Bayley, C M, *Empire and Intelligence*, (Cambridge: Cambridge University Press, 1996).

3   Boehmer, Elleke, *Colonial and Postcolonial Literature*, (Oxford and New York: Oxford University Press, 1995).

4   Brantlinger, Patrick, *Rule of Darkness: British Literature and Imperialism: 1830-1914*, (Cornell University Press, 1988).

5   Bristow, Joseph, *Empire Boys: Adventures in a Man's World*, (New York & London: Harper Collins, 1991).

6   Embree, Ainslie, ed, *1857 In India: Mutiny or War of Independence*, (Boston: Heath Books, 1963).

7   Freud, Sigmund, Reprint, *Civilization and its Discontents*, Translated by James Strachey, (New York: Norton, 1961).

8   Foucault, Michel, *Discipline and Punish: The Birth of the Prison*, English translation by Alan Sheridan, (London and New York: Vintage Books, 1979).

9   Hyam, Ronald, *Britain's Imperial Century, 1815-1914*, (New York and London: Macmillan, 1993).

10   Kaye, John W, *The Administration of the East India Company*, (London: Oxford University Press, 1853).

11   Kloss, Boden C, *Andamans and Nicobars: The Narrative of a Cruise in the Schooner "Terrapin,"* (New Delhi: Vivek Publishing House, 1971).

12   Macaulay, T B, "Speech in the House of Commons," 2nd Feburary 1835, in G W Young, ed, *Speeches*, (Oxford: Oxford University Press, 1935).

13   Mathur, L P, *History of the Andaman and Nicobar Islands, 1756-1966*, (New Delhi: Sterling Publishers, 1968).

14   Mill, James, *History of British India*, Vols 1-6, (London: 1820), reprint (New York: Chelsea House, 1968).

15   Savarkar, V D, *The Story of My Transportation for Life: A Biography of Black Days in Andamans*, Translated by V N Naik, (Bombay: Sadbhakti Publishers, 1950).

16   Singh, Iqbal N, *The Andaman Story*, (New Delhi: Vikas Publishing House, 1978).

17   Sinha, Bijoy Kumar, *Andaman: The Indian Bastille*, (Allahabad: Pustak Mahal, 1939).

18   Solzhenitsyn, Aleksandr I, *The Gulag Archipelago, 1918-1956 (Vols.I-IV)*, Translated by Thomas P Whitney, (New York and London: Harper Row Publishers, 1974).

19   Tegart, Charles, *Notes on Andaman Enquiry*, File no.293 Govt of Bengal Intelligence Branch of the Police Dept, 1913.

20   Tegart, Kathleen, [unpublished manuscript], *Memoir of an Indian Policeman* (containing entries from C A Tegart's Diaries), India Office Library, London.

21   Wedgewood, J, "Hell on Earth," *Searchlight* (6ᵗʰ February 1921): 4, (Originally published in *The Daily Telegraph*, London).

22   Wick, Robin, *British Imperialism: Gold, God, Glory*, (New York & London: Holt, Rhinehart, Winston, 1963).

23   Wurgaft, L D, *The Imperial Imagination*, (Middletown, Conn.: Wesleyan University Press, 1983).

PROPAGANDA AS TRAVELOGUE:
A STUDY OF KATHERINE MAYO'S *MOTHER INDIA*

MOHAMMED ZAHEER BASHA

In the year 1926, Katherine Mayo (1868-1940), by then a journalist and writer of some repute in the USA, visited India for a few months to "see what a volunteer, unsubsidized, uncommitted and unattached could observe of common things in human life."[1] *Mother India* was the result of this journey. The book became a bestseller in the English-speaking world and was seen as an important critique on Hindu civilization and Indian political aspirations. In five parts and over thirty chapters, the author gives an account of her avowedly disinterested travel in lucid, and sometimes charged, prose. Beginning with a lurid description of a ritual animal sacrifice at the Kalighat in Calcutta she moves on to delineate – and at times dissect – the gender inequality, child marriage, the caste system, Hindu and Muslim political concerns, the relevance of Gandhi and the Congress, the role of Christian missionaries, and of the virtues and the practical indispensability of the British Raj. A close reading of the book, however, reveals a very interested outlook, as she tries to fit in all information – and quite an amount of misinformation – into a preconceived structure of beliefs. The irony is that, in the first chapter entitled "The Argument," Mayo expresses her dissatisfaction over the "hazy notions" that the average American could at best get from, among other sources, "professional propagandists out of one camp or another," as the reason for her decision to travel to India for a first hand encounter.[2]

That the book should have elicited strong reactions from contemporary Indians and from those sympathetic to India was as much due to its huge success in the West as to the flagrant nature of – what amounted to – imperialist propaganda in and around the book.[3] We need also to recall that the year in which this book was published, that is 1927, was the same year in which the Indian nationalists were agitating against the all-white Simon Commission to assert the Indians' right to represent themselves. In that context, Mayo's efforts to prove the inability of Indians for self-rule was seen by a great majority of Indian public men as imperialist propaganda.

The very title of the book seems to have a tongue-in-cheek connotation, as C S Ranga Iyer observed in his rejoinder, *Father India*.[4] We are aware as to how, to the freedom fighters, India was a politico-religious mother-image. And the frontline of nationalists, as we know, was comprised mainly of upper caste Hindus who were, to the British, dangerously articulate, with the Indian National Congress as their forum. Mayo presents the retrogressive orthodoxy of sections of this group as fully representative of the society under her scrutiny. This was seen by several of her Indian critics as exemplifying the imperialist mindset.

Her one and almost only source on Hinduism is Abbe Dubois' *Hindu Manners, Customs and Ceremonies*, a book notorious for its interested analysis of Hinduism. The Abbe had escaped the Great Revolution in France, on his own testimony, owing to his religious and political views. As a proselytizing priest in India, once again on his own admission, he proved disastrous, and to serve Christianity in another way, he chose to write the book.[5] In his Preface he writes:

> There is one motive, which, above all others, has influenced my determination [to write the book]. It struck me that a faithful picture of the wickedness and incongruities of polytheism and idolatry would by its very ugliness help greatly to set off the beauties and perfections of Christianity ...[6]

Now, no one disinterestedly curious about a religion would have chosen the Abbe, with his avowed interests, as a source. But Mayo, obviously, found in him a most convenient source. The fact that the Abbe retired with a pension from the East India Company for his "many services rendered in India" must have been a point in favour to the author, whose pro-imperialist leanings were well known since the publication of her book, *The Isle of Fear: An Examination of America's Task in the Philippines (1925)* in which she had argued against any move by the American government towards granting any measure of autonomy to the Filipinos.[7]

Basing her observations on this dubious source, Mayo says, inter alia, that Indian mothers usually encourage premature sexual indulgences in their children, that boys were gladly drafted to be temple prostitutes, that eating dung is all in a day's work to a Hindu, that pre-pubertal sex in marriage was considered normal, that unescorted women in India were almost always raped, that most of the young widows walked the streets, that the preoccupation with sex and sexual symbols pre-empted possibilities of constructive and creative pursuits, et cetera. Much was said in hurt and rage in the written responses to these contents of the book, many times taking the form of look-at-your-own-society-before-you-dare-to-speak-of-us. Considering that the twenties were a turbulent phase in

America, it gave ample opportunities to her Indian critics to return the compliments. Perhaps anticipating this line of attack, she states at the end of the very first chapter "The Argument":

> Outside agencies working for the moral welfare of the Indian seem often to have adopted the method of encouraging their beneficiary to dwell on his own merits and to harp upon others' short-comings, rather than to face his faults and conquer them.[8]

The author's stated concern is, however, belied by the value-judgemental tone of much of the narrative.

For instance, after giving lurid pictures of a day's happenings at the Kali temple at Kalighat , she quotes an English theosophist as saying, "[O]nly the lowest and the most ignorant of Indians are Kali worshippers." She quotes, "[A] most learned and distinguished of Bangalee Brahmans" who refutes the theosophist's observation by claiming that "hundreds and thousands of Brahmans everywhere worship Kali."[9]

For Mayo, this statement comes from the horse's mouth and helps her reinforce the stereotype of the degenerate Hindu Brahmin. And all this, of course, presumes the "wickedness" of ritualistic worship of the goddess.

The author's solid belief in the norms of her culture as ideal and unassailable and her disdain for any variation is unambiguously stated. Whenever she speaks of religious rituals, gender relations, sexuality or social organization, what seem like her racial and conservative attitudes are revealed, in fact, as a standard tool for the justification of colonial rule. In constructing the *other*, she can make allegations which are as follows:

> *In fact, so far are they from seeing good and evil as we see good and evil,* that the mother, high caste or low caste, will practise upon her children – the girl "to make her sleep well," the boy

87

"to make him manly"– an abuse which the boy, at least, is apt to continue daily for the rest of his life."(sic)(Emphasis mine)[10]

Not surprisingly, such sections of the book attracted outraged responses in the rejoinders from several Indian public men. C S Ranga Iyer, for instance, in his *Father India,* sought to take home the attack by extensively quoting American sources on teenage pregnancies in America.[11] In the narrative, the "us" and "them" attitude is there throughout and comes clearly to the surface at times. Writing of the Hindu attitude towards sex symbols – and by implication, social attitude towards sexuality – with reference to the 1923 Geneva convention on the "suppression of the circulation of and traffic in obscene publications," and the modified adaptation of the same by the Indian Legislature, she observes,

> [I]ts unqualified enactment would have wrought havoc with the religious belongings, the ancient traditions and customs and the priestly prerogatives dear to the Hindu majority.[12]

Here the author's obviously distancing the "civilized" West from an Eastern culture she considers incompatible with "decent" laws. These constructs of "us" and "them" are grounded in a sense of racial superiority, an example of which is best seen when, journeying across the north, she comes upon a marching troop of English soldiers and gushes: "Tramp-tramp-a-marching detachment of the Second Battalion Royal Fusiliers – open-faced, bright-skinned English lads, smart and keen – an incredible sight in that setting."[13] The racial pride and consciousness of superiority hardly need elucidation here.

In the Indian context, racial prejudice translates itself into religious prejudice. Speaking of the disdainful attitude of upper caste Hindus towards Christian converts she says: "But of the converts of the third generation many persons are found to say that they are the hope of India."[14] It is so strongly reminiscent of the view of Abbe Dubois, her source on Hinduism, who held that the Hindu can be "saved" only when he gives up his religion and embraces Christianity. In the colonial context, the people who held the reins of power obviously understood the political benefits of conversions in legitimizing exploitation and knew the value of men like the Abbe. Mayo, however, chose not to probe the issue.

The unkindest cut, however, comes in the form of a frankly political punch. Here is Mayo, describing the nature of the East India Company:

> A human enterprise covering two centuries of human progress, the name of the East India Company was sometimes dimmed by mistaken judgement or by unfit agents. Some of these were overbearing, some tactless, some wavering, one or two were base, and a few succumbed to the temptation of graft. Of their defects, however, not a little nonsense is spun.[15]

This admiration for a "human enterprise covering two centuries of human progress" and the implied castigation of those who are, to the author, ungrateful, conveys, in a very unequivocal way, the historical nature of her perception and her imperialist attitude.

Mayo uses every conceivable and inconceivable means to force her point through. She twists Tagore's words to prove him an apologist for the institution of child-marriage by selectively and misleadingly quoting him from his essay "The Indian Ideal of Marriage."[16] She gives this as his considered opinion on the subject:

> For the purpose of marriage, spontaneous love is unreliable; its proper cultivation should yield the best results ... and the cultivation should begin before marriage. Therefore, from the earliest years the husband as an idea is held up before our girls, in verse and story, through ceremonial and worship. When at length they get the husband, he is to them not a

person but a principle, like loyalty, patriotism, or such other abstractions.[17]

These words of Tagore, it must be noted, were preceded by: "these must have been the lines of argument, in regard to married love, pursued in our country."[18]

Gandhi is extensively quoted whenever his words are an articulation of his frank diagnosis of social ills, with Mayo always remembering to leave out the part speaking of effort and hope. This, as a strategy, is no doubt rhetorically useful but unacceptable when a work claims to represent the truth. Gandhi understated it when he observed in his reaction to the book:

> Any person who collects extracts from a reformer's diary, tears them from their context and proceeds to condemn, on the strength of these, the people in whose midst the reformer had worked, would get no hearing from sane and unbiased readers.[19]

Unfortunately, however, Mayo did get a hearing, a good one at that, in the English-speaking world. She obviously appealed as much to those who benignly believed in the "white man's burden" as to those who were less sophisticatedly racist.

The author gives an impression of fairplay by writing of her arguments with Indians. This is, characteristically, only apparent. She contrives highly insufficient and weak rhetoric for the side arguing with her, or chooses to put on record only those reactions that serve the purpose of her rhetoric. For instance, when she laments the educated Indian youth wasting their time in "idle talk" and suggests that it would be better if they went to rural areas to do some constructive work instead, she has one young political leader, speaking for others as well, saying: "[P]erhaps, but talk, also is work. Talk is now the only work. Nothing else can be done till we push the alien out of India."[20] She then quotes, on the same page, "an American long resident in India, deeply and sympathetically interested in the Indian" as saying, "[I]t was a crime to teach them to be clerks, lawyers and politicians till they'd been taught to raise food."[21] On the one hand, the author derides the proclivity of the Indian for futile talk and concurs with the view that the English system of education is responsible to a great extent for the political discontent and on the other, would see no wrong whatsoever in the way the Raj had worked/was working. At this point the whole issue of the disaffection towards the empire, supposedly induced by English education, offers itself for a rational analysis. However, perhaps with good reason, the author chooses not to take up the analysis.

Mayo also accuses Indians of being habitual liars. In her own words:

The Indian may be a devoted "seeker after truth" in the sense of metaphysical speculation; he may be of a splendid candour in dealing with most parts of most subjects of which you speak together. And yet he may from time to time embed in the midst of his frank speech statements easily susceptible of proof and totally at variance with facts.[22]

In her quest to know the truth about liars, Mayo speaks to a European who has been a resident of India for a long time. She asks him, "Why do men of high position make false statements and then name in support of documents which, when I dig them out, either fail to touch the subject at all, or else prove the statements to be false?" And the European replies: "Because to the Hindu, nothing is false that he wants to believe. Or all matters being nothingness, all statements concerning it are lies. Therefore he may blamelessly choose the lie that serves his purpose ..."[23]

She goes on to cite further proof of the Indian's degenerate traits:

Inertia, helplessness, lack of initiative and originality, lack of staying power and of sustained loyalties, sterility of enthusiasm, weakness of life-vigour itself – all are traits that truly characterise the Indian not only of today, but of long-past history. All, furthermore, will continue to characterise him, in increasing degrees, until he admits their causes and with his own two hands uproots them ... And his arraignments of outside elements, past, present, or to come, serve only to deceive his own mind to put off the day of his deliverence.[24]

In other words, for Indians, blaming the Raj for anything whatsoever, and seeking political freedom amounted to an escapist indulgence. The untenability of this view hardly needs elaboration, as economic critiques of English imperialism were well known by this time.

Many contemporary critics of the book noted, but thought it wise not to elaborate on Mayo's soft treading on Muslim toes, perhaps because of the political climate then. She projects the upper-caste Hindu as the cause of all disaffection in the country, what with his caste-dominated Congress claiming to speak for all Indians. We are aware how the British Raj was patronizing communal politics. Mayo, following the lead, gets to work pretty seriously to do her bit. She uses, among other things, the anti-Brahmin feelings in the Madras province, the alleged faith of the people in the goodness of English officers over the mainly upper-caste Indian ones, the words of an North West Frontier Province (NWFP) Pathan against Hindus, to make out a case against her target.

With her sense of racial superiority, Mayo had no more reason to love the Muslim than she had to love the Hindu. However, that he is monotheistic unlike the Hindu seems, to her, a point in the Muslim's favour. Note, of course, her observation: "Literate or illiterate, the Mohammedan is a passionate monotheist. 'There is but one God.' His mosques are clear of images. His frequent daily prayer is offered straight to the invisible One omnipotent ..."[25] As is obvious, a certain amount of value-judgement regarding religious practice is involved here.

Mayo exceeds herself in making out a kind of two-nation theory from her "observations." Towards this end, the representation of the Muslim is consistent vis-à-vis the Hindu and his concerns (both of the communal stereotype). She also projects Muslim communalist concerns as genuine and valid. There is, of course, a build-up in the rhetoric to make the conclusions reached sound tenable.

For instance, giving details of the Legislative Assembly debates of 1925 on the proposed Age of Consent bill, the author writes, "upon the unfruitful circlings of the Hindus breaks, once and again, a voice from the hardy North."[26] And this is the voice of a *Muslim* member representing the NWFP whose argument is that since the government could do little about child-marriages, it would be futile to seek to enforce a particular age of consent for consummation. This is placed amidst quotes from the most conservative Hindu legislators, conveniently ignoring that there were less unreasonable and even liberal speakers who were trying to get the bill passed. The way Mayo represents it, the point here seems not so much the issue being debated as is the – just – cynicism of a Muslim member over an issue of great concern and even embarrassment to his Hindu colleagues.

Again, in her account of the Bombay Legislative Council discussion on a proposed bill to coerce local boards to admit "untouchable" children into schools, in the midst of clever stalling talk by some orthodox Hindu members, a Muslim legislator from Sind is approvingly quoted as "striking the practical note" when he observes that since the upper-castes were ever so reluctant to treat the "untouchables" as fellow human beings, they would have no right to protest if these people turned to Christianity or Islam for succour.[27] This observation too, no doubt, smacks of cynicism and disdain. Nevertheless, these serve Mayo's purpose of playing off one community against the other. The point here is "who is saying it" rather than what's being said. In a social context of uncertain communal relations, Mayo must have realized the effectiveness of such rhetoric. The chapter "Behind the Veil" is mainly an indictment of the purdah practising Hindu upper castes. Even there, the Muslim escapes the brunt of the attack though the system was also prevalent among the Muslims.

On the other hand, there are sections in the book, for example the chapter "Sons of the Prophet" which gives an image of the Muslim that is in full conformity both to the self-projection of the most rabidly communal Muslim and to the impression sought to be reinforced by his Hindu counterpart. The basic point here serves Mayo's purpose of playing off one community against the other and depicts the utter incompatibility of these two "peoples." A number of pages in the same section are devoted to the representations made by various Muslim organizations to Montague, Secretary of State, in 1917, pleading for the continuance of the Raj citing the fear of Hindu dominance in case the British should decide to go some day. The author, in consonance with her principles, just does not try to examine how representative these bodies were. We know that in the 1936 elections, the Muslim League secured only 4.8% of the total Muslim vote. If the Muslim organizations were really as representative as Mayo made them out to be, 1937 would have been a different year.

At one point, speaking of the Muslim, she says:

> Always an internationalist rather than a nationalist, all over India the Mohammedan is saying today: "We are foreigners, conquerors, fighting men. What if our numbers are small! Is it numbers or men that count? When the British go, *we* shall rule India."[28]

There is a contradiction in the rhetoric here. If, as she seems to say, quoting the Muslim representations to Montague, the Muslims felt insecure about the prospect of the British leaving and the Hindus taking over, how then could her statement be true? Should not the Muslims desire the end of the Raj so that they could take over and "rule the Hindus?" Mayo was, evidently, carried away by the force of her enthusiasm to prove her "point."

The author's warped account of the Moplah uprising in 1921 takes the cake among her travesties of truth about political conditions and processes in India. She would have us believe that the Khilafat agitation to the Moplah meant the overthrow of the Raj and the establishment of the rule of Islam in India. She gives the impression that the Moplah uprising was an anti-Hindu affair from beginning to end. This flies in the face of known facts. Modern history classifies it as an agrarian unrest that went haywire. The Moplahs, even before 1921, had a history of such unrests on smaller scales. In 1921 also, it began as a protest against the rock-renting practices of the jenmies, the mostly upper-class landlords. The Khilafat agitation was allied to it after the Congress took up the issue. The violence began as the result of official indiscretion and apathy, and the first targets were the government buildings, and then the more notorious among the jenmies and also pro-government Moplahs. And the English reprisal that followed, with its unmatched brutality, finally drove the unled Moplahs into a phase of anti-Hindu actions.

Through such a lopsided account of this tragic event, Mayo sought to strengthen the theory of communal incompatibility. This account also serves her to discredit the man, Gandhi, and his principles, blaming the violence on the Khilafat initiative taken by him.

The New Statesman, in its review, appreciatively called the book "One of the most powerful defences of the British Raj that has ever been written."[29] Though highly partisan, *The New Statesman* seems to have reflected the general attitude of most white readers. And if the book turned out to be such a bestseller, it must have been because of – the racist reasons apart – its racy style and lucid representation, notwithstanding the dubious basis of its assumptions and observations. Gandhi, referring to the success of the book, was to observe: "Though she represents a class of sensational writers in the West, it is a class that, I flatter myself with the belief, is on the wane."[30] Obviously, the sensationalist writer is yet to be found dispensable, especially in the West, and it may be worthwhile to look into Mayo's rhetorical devices that made the book so talked about.

We have already noted the tongue-in-cheek tone of the book's very title. Chapter titling too is no exception, being loaded with sarcasm. For instance, the chapters dealing with child-marriage and its consequences are titled "Early to Marry and Early to Die," "Spades are Spades," "The Earthly God," "Wages of Sin," and so on. The chapter dealing with educated Indians' yearning for public office is called "Give Me Office or Give Me Death." Of course, the sarcasm is not limited to titling alone, and is specially used whenever the author thinks she has an irrefutable point. And when she is not so sure, she tries to make up through emotionally charged narration.

In her description of the reception given to the Prince of Wales in 1921 in the background of the Congress boycott decision, she has uncontrollable Indians chanting, "Hail to the Prince! Let me only see my Prince! Let me only see my Prince just once before I die," and "Look! Look! Behold, the Light, the Light!" along the way of the royal motorcade.[31]

The ridicule extends to Indian political and cultural identities framed as obsessions with its past "Golden Age" and the tendency to blame its end on external sources. Thus she observes:

> Or again, the accuser first paints a picture of an idyllic land, distinguished by science, philosophy and pastoral grace, then suddenly confronts his hearer with the challenge: can you show me, in all India, any remnant of that life? No? Exactly.

Then, if it exists nowhere, does it not follow that Britain must have destroyed it?[32]

Such accusers, wherever the author found them, help her in holding up to – what seems deserved – ridicule any critique of the Raj. One cannot be certain about the authenticity or otherwise of such encounters but one can see that the effect sought to be produced fits in into her ideological framework.

Mayo's own interpretation of the Indian past and present is, however, different. After giving a brief history of crime that she believes was perpetrated on India by the Muslim "invaders" and selfish Hindu chieftains, the author speaks of the "great human enterprise that the East India Company was" and refers to the year 1858 in these words:

> Shabby, threadbare, sick and poor, old Mother India stood at last on the brink of another world and turned blind eyes toward the strange new flag above her head. It carried then, as it carries today, a pledge that is, to her, incredible. How can she, the victim and slave of all recorded time, either hope or believe that her latest master brings her the gift of constructive service, democracy and the weal of the common people?[33]

The Millennium, for India, Mayo seems to be saying, arrived in that year!   ~

To conclude, one may quote the author at her reasonable best:

> Now, in the name of fairplay, it cannot be too strongly emphasised that this characteristic, this point of view, this different evaluation, constitutes not necessarily inferiority, but certainly a difference, like the colour of the skin. Yet as a difference involved in the heart of human intercourse, it must constantly be reckoned with and understood; else that intercourse will often and needlessly crash.[34]

Even if accepted at face value, it can still be asserted, from what we have seen so far, that her own attempts at a human intercourse *did* crash, and the seeds of the failure must lie in her barely concealed attitude of racial arrogance and impatience. After all, she came not to see, but to confirm and damn.

Notes

1 Katherine Mayo, *Mother India*, (London: Jonathan Cape, 1927), 20.

2 Katherine Mayo, *Mother* India, 20. "What does the average American actually know about India? That Mr Gandhi lives there; also tigers. His further ideas, if such he has, resolve themselves into more or less hazy notions more or less unconsciously absorbed from professional propagandists out of one camp or another."

3 Manoranjan Jha, *Katherine Mayo and India*, (New Delhi: Peoples Publishing House, 1971) gives documented evidence of government patronage to Mayo during her research and the propagandist use of the book later by the media and the establishment.

4 C S Ranga Iyer, *Father India*, (London: Selwyn & Blount Ltd., 1927), "[S]atirically, the American tourist (Mayo) calls her book *Mother India*, in whose name the English-hating Nationalist appeals to the masses."

5 Abbe Dubois, *Letters on the state of Christianity in India*, (London, 1823), in which he writes of his conviction, after thirty two years of missionary work, that the conversion of Hindus, with "their deep rooted prejudices of centuries," was impossible under the conditions then existing.

6 Abbe Dubois, page number not available.

7 In this book, Mayo's basic point is that, except for the politicians, the Filipinos were neither interested in, nor ready, for political freedom. Katherine Mayo, *The Isles of Fear: An Examination of America's Task in the Philippines*, as quoted in Manoranjan Jha, *Katherine Mayo and India*, (New Delhi: Peoples Publishing House, 1971).

8 Katherine Mayo, *Mother India*, 26.

9 Katherine Mayo, *Mother* India, 19. Neither the "English theosophist" nor the "Bengalee Brahman" is named by the author.

10 Katherine Mayo, *Mother India*, 33.

11 C S Ranga Iyer quotes extensively from Judge Ben Lindsey's *Revolt of Modern Youth, a* deeply concerned social work on sexual promiscuity and teenage pregnancies in the USA in the twenties.

12 C S Ranga Iyer, *Father India*, 32.

13 C S Ranga Iyer, *Father India*, 67.
14 C S Ranga Iyer, *Father India*, 152.
15 C S Ranga Iyer, *Father India*, 257-58.
16 Rabindranath Tagore, "The Indian Ideal of Marriage," in Hermann Keyserling, ed, *The Book of Marriage: A New Interpretation by 24 Leaders of Contemporary Thought*, (New York: Harcourt, Brace and Co., 1926).
17 Rabindranath Tagore, "The Indian Ideal of Marriage," 75.
18 Rabindranath Tagore, "The Indian Ideal of Marriage," 112-13.
19 Gandhi, *Young India*, 15th September 1927.
20 Katherine Mayo, *Mother India*, 200.
21 Katherine Mayo, *Mother India*, 200.
22 Katherine Mayo, *Mother India*, 272.
23 Katherine Mayo, *Mother India*, 273.
24 Katherine Mayo, *Mother India*, 24
25 Katherine Mayo, *Mother India*, 290.
26 Katherine Mayo, *Mother India*, 47
27 Katherine Mayo, *Mother India*, 146.
28 Katherine Mayo, *Mother India*, 303-304.
29 *The New Statesman*, 16th July 1927.
30 Gandhi, *Young India*, 15th September 1927.
31 Katherine Mayo, *Mother India*, 199.
32 Katherine Mayo, *Mother India*, 243.
33 Katherine Mayo, *Mother India*, 259.
34 Katherine Mayo, *Mother India*, 274.

References

1 Mayo, Katherine, *Mother India*, (London: Jonathan Cape, 1927).
2 Dubois, J A Abbe, *Hindu Manners, Customs and Ceremonies*, (Oxford: Clarendon, 1924).
3 Iyer, C S Ranga, *Father India*, (London: Selwyn & Blount Ltd., 1927).
4 Jha, Manoranjan, *Katherine Mayo and India*, (New Delhi: Peoples Publishing House, 1971).
5 Keyserling, Herman, *Book of Marriage: A New Interpretation by 24 Leaders of Contemporary Thought*, (New York: Harcourt, Brace and Co., 1926).
6 Natarajan, K, *Mother India: A Rejoinder*, (Madras: G A Natesan & Co., 1927).
7 Chandra, Bipan, et al., *India's Struggle for Independence*, (Delhi: Penguin Books, 1989).

CONSTITUTIVE CONTRADICTIONS:
TRAVEL WRITING AND CONSTRUCTION OF NATIVE WOMEN IN COLONIAL INDIA

SINDHU MENON

Both as object of colonial historiography and as subject of insurgency,
the ideological constructions keep the male dominant. If in the context
of colonial production, the subaltern has no history and cannot speak,
the subaltern as female is even more deeply in shadow. [1]

It has become a commonplace of postcolonial criticism today to treat as a convenient myth the notion that imperial edifices are either impermeable or monolithic by nature. The shades of variation found among contemporary representations clearly indicate that we are not dealing with a uniform monolithic structure, but rather with a collage or jigsaw puzzle, where the faultlines remain visible despite the surface appearance of a wholeness. This paper argues that these differences, these "inconsistencies" within the colonial paradigm were not extraneous "mistakes" that weakened the structure. There is evidence to indicate that at an ontological or epistemological level, strategic textual discourses that aim at control *cannot* totally succeed in their project of glossing over history. There are bound to be, as inevitable adjuncts of discursivity itself, lacunae where more dialogic versions of the constituent transactions inscribe themselves.

However, at a pragmatic level, the inconsistencies were actually "constitutive" elements of the structure itself. Far from weakening the working force of the imperial network, they furthered its efficacy by making it possible to accommodate political and theoretical positions of apparent wide divergence without seeming incongruity. This argument can be illustrated by examining almost any particular facet of colonial representation. As a particularly productive example, I have selected the representation of Indian women in early European (mainly British) travel texts.

The situation of the woman in formerly colonized societies is doubly complex since her identity has been submerged on two distinct fronts – that of colonialism based on race, and that of patriarchy based on gender. The notion of "double colonisation, i.e., that women in formerly colonised societies were *doubly* colonised by both imperial and patriarchal ideologies"[2] is significant in this context. It is also necessary to note that the situation is extra complex when the representation was carried out by the *women* of a colonizing race, since they were inscribed as "colonizer" by race and as "colonized" by gender.

For the white woman, the Indian woman is a racial "Other" (and also a potential sexual rival). But there is also a simultaneous uneasy identification at the level of gender. The complexities engendered by this double bind will be considered in the latter part of this analysis. No precise answers are available for the vexing question, which of the two, race or gender, should be given prominence. However, I do attempt to trace out the intricately entangled strands of this "alliance." The larger part of the texts examined here are the productions, therefore, of British women travellers. Of course, representative texts by British men, as well as those of a few non-British travellers are examined.

CONSTITUTIVE CONTRADICTIONS

Roy Porter and G S Rousseau, in *Exoticism and Enlightenment*, have discussed the "exoticizing" process:

Containing an element of the forbidden, though without its correlate, the abominable, the exotic is that realm of the excluded which is not absolutely prohibited, but merely signposted by danger lights. It has equivalent status in the geocultural realm to the daydream in the psychodynamic. It is marked by frisson more than fear.[3]

The representation of Indian women was the primary site of such a European "exoticizing" of India. In colonialist iconography, the Indian woman occupied a much more complicated position than her male counterparts. We have a very powerful discourse that posits an image of the Oriental woman as the archetypal Other, alluring and dangerous precisely because of her very Otherness. At the same time, the persuasive and pervasive notion of the entire colonial enterprise as a civilizing mission rendered it imperative that colonized women be also represented as an oppressed and silenced group who dumbly looked towards the colonizers for rescue and help. We also have to contend with the wholesale "feminization" of the colony as such, which created "feminine men" and in the process rendered the "real" woman's situation even more ambivalent. Questions can also be raised about the presence of a systematic and ordered suppression of native women's voices, a project into which the female members of the ruling race were also co-opted.

Was the Indian woman the ideal subject of embodied femininity or the passive object of oppression? In keeping with their need to view colonialism as a lofty self-sacrificing mission, the male writers, even when they confessed on occasion to a physical attraction for native women, usually followed it up with a qualification or ambiguous disclaimer. James Forbes' comment that "the Hindoo women when young are delicate and beautiful, *so far as we can reconcile the idea of beauty with the olive complexion*" is a useful illustration of this trend (emphasis mine).[4] Yet another type of disclaimer is "to damn with faint praise," as demonstrated by Richard Burton's comment: "Some of the [Hindu] women are by no means deficient in personal charms."[5]

However, sexual attraction towards native women was also combined with a fear of their unbridled libido that seemed to threaten the colonizer's defining masculinity. The Nair women of Kerala were specifically focussed on in this context, since the Marumakkathayam (matrilineal) system they practised rendered them seemingly beyond subjugation. The claims made by travellers regarding the sexual excesses of these women were incredible in their exaggerations. Varthema claims that all "marriages were consummated by the age of ten," and "there were very few virgins among either sex at the age of seven or eight."[6] Van Linschoten goes a step further by asserting that Nair girls are not only capable of sexual activity by the age of seven, but that they are so aggressive even at that age as to pose actual physical threats to men.[7] Varthema also records an instance where a Nair merchant requested Varthema's European friend to "deflower" his young bride as it was an honour for the husband, according to the native customs. The most telling part of the anecdote is the final sentence, where Varthema, supposedly speaking for the young bride, says, "[T]ruly the lady would have desired that the first night had lasted a month."[8] The suggestion is that only the truly masculine white man can satisfy the dangerously lascivious native woman. The native man is just not man enough.

Varthema also comes up with a theory (for which I have not been able to trace any authentic source) that the Nair women "intend nothing but their lust, and think that if they die virgins, they shall never enter into Paradise."[9] This must have indeed seemed a

103

frightening inversion of the Christian religion's emphasis on the sacred nature of virginity. However, despite this fear of unbridled native female sexuality, and in spite of the rhetorical disclaimers, a distinct exotic and erotic attraction towards native women still contrives to emerge from these accounts.

Indeed, the threat posed by the sexual allure of the native woman is a constant irritant, which is also a major motivation behind certain white women travellers' jocular/contemptuous dismissal of even the possibility of a "successful" miscegenetic relationship. Isabella Fane comments, in a highly sarcastic tone, which does not quite mask the anxiety:

> Among the presents for the Governor General, there was a tiger which has been nursed and brought up by a native woman. Woman and all is presented. As Sir C- has the reputation of not caring for colour in his little amours, she may be acceptable.[10]

Male travellers often give lyrical accounts of the appearance and appeal of the Indian women. James Forbes' verdict is that, on the whole, Indian women approximate far more closely to the ideal conception of femininity than their British counterparts. Though he speaks of the British duty of "liberating" Indian women, Forbes often gets carried away by his version of docile, malleable femininity and argues for the patriarchal system, that the seclusion of Indian women has many advantages that adequately compensate the loss of liberty. The implication is that precisely because of their secluded life and the docility that it engenders, Indian women are ideally feminine creatures with whom a liaison would be enjoyable.

This idea is further developed in references to the "natural" Indian woman as opposed to the "artificial" European ladies:

> You may talk of your French woman's walk – it may be

pretty – indeed, it is so; but is it natural? She goes pitter-patting along as though she feared at each step to burst her shoe. My *Indian daughter of nature* has no shoe to burst, but she plants a very pretty bare foot with precision yet lightness, and floats past, unencumbered with the weighty vase, which her slender neck seems almost too fragile to support.[11]

Of course, such open commendation, patriarchal or otherwise, was not an *officially* acceptable view for any member of the ruling race. So, the attraction exercised by the native woman was often underplayed by rhetorical references to their intellectual deprivation. Still, despite this anticipatory bail, the undercurrent of attraction comes through loud and clear. This seems to be the spur behind the near-total tendency among British women travel writers to either ignore or reduce to slighting references in passing the physical appearance of the Indian woman. They also emphasize the vast cultural gulf that *should* prevent Indian women from being suitable mates for the "civilized" Englishmen.

Emily Eden refers to the extreme "seclusion" of Indian women only to conclude that they must be boring companions indeed. Isabella Fane is seriously worried that her nephew may grow up "very black" because he had a native wet nurse. Eliza Fay sets forth a blanket condemnation of Indian women – in sharp contrast to their portrayals as "daughters of nature" – for using too much "art" and thereby spoiling even the little beauty they naturally possess. Interestingly, these same women writers are also fierce champions for the "emancipation" of the monolithic configuration of "the Indian woman." However, the line is firmly drawn at accepting a liaison between individual Indian women and White men. The ambivalent attitude of the colonizing men towards the charms of the native women must have helped in the rigid construction of this notion. Actually, the White women did not have much to be really anxious about, however erotic an appeal native women may have had – "The lure of female sexuality [was] never far from the threat of female power."[12]

The notion of emancipating the native woman was fundamental to the discourse of colonialism as a civilizing mission. The "liberty" and the "protection" accorded to native women functioned as a graph for plotting the success or otherwise of this mission. As Gayatri Spivak points out, the perpetual refrain was that of "white men saving brown women from brown men."[13] This confers a very limited subjectivity on the native male as the agent of oppression, but completely freezes the native woman as the object of both native oppression and colonizer's rescue. In the Indian context, the prohibition of the custom of Sati is the ideal example of the colonial succor of the colonized woman. Nearly all the travel texts included in this paper contain at least one detailed reference to Sati, either an eyewitness report or a secondhand account.

Despite the official commitment to abolishing Sati, a certain ambivalence can be seen, at least in the texts produced by *men* travellers. In the first place, the element of the exotic spectacle involved in Sati seems to have been a severe temptation.

> [The crowd] suggested that it was certainly a *suttee*, or burning of a Hindoo widow that was about to take place. Though feeling a great repugnance for painful sights, I determined to *avail myself of an opportunity* which seldom *offers itself to a native of Europe of SEEING one of the most remarkable customs of the East.*[14]

James Forbes includes a long eyewitness account of Sati in which he finds himself compelled to admire the "heroism" of the Sati. His only regret is that she "did not have Christian morality to teach her the futility of such an act."[15] The entire scene is described as a grand spectacle. As Kate Teltscher points out:

> As an erasure of the widow's sexuality, Sati bears a distant

affinity to the ideal life of chastity and fidelity to the memory of a deceased husband prescribed for seventeenth century English Widows."[16]

Hardly surprising, therefore, that Englishmen, despite the official attitude of disapproval, had mixed responses to Sati.

The colonizers as a whole did stress the need for abolishing Sati. But the European men were susceptible to the heroic and romantic associations of the rite, far more so than the women, who regarded it totally indignantly and angrily. It is possible that the implicit suggestion that the British men were ready on occasion to glorify Sati was a disconcerting thought, which led the women writers to take all possible occasions for condemnation. Sati, for them, was not just an erotic or barbaric practice. It was also a potential threat.

Emily Eden refers to the Sati committed by two of Ranjit Singh's Queens, whom she calls "those poor dear Ranees," and adds, "they would have given it up if they had any hope of kind treatment."[17] Eliza Fay argues with feminist zeal that "this ritual [Sati] is but part of the schemes of men in most countries to invent a sufficient number of rules to render the women totally subservient to their authority."[18] But she also adds:

I cannot avoid smiling when I hear some gentlemen bring forward the conduct of the Hindu women as a test of superior character. I am well aware that so much are we the slaves of habit that were it necessary for a woman's reputation to burn herself in England, many a one who had accepted a husband merely for the sake of an establishment ... and rendered his life uncomfortable to its close, would yet mount the funeral pyre with all the imaginable decency and die with a heroic display of fortitude.[19]

The issue of Sati, though most prominent, was not the only issue in the discourse of saving native women. The susceptibility of Indian women to "holy Men" – who are uniformly presented as sex-crazed imposters – the Devadasi system, and the lack of education as well as the retarding seclusion are also stressed. More than as systems open to reform, Indian religions are presented as being ontologically oppressive and thereby to be eradicated. Sir Thomas Herbert describes in almost pornographic terms a ceremony where a new bride is violated by the "bodkin" of an idol.[20] In a paradoxical formulation, it is superstition that is behind these rites, but the Indian men are not just superstitious; they are positively sadistic. The voyeurism of the European traveller, however, is coded only in terms of reformative and intellectual curiosity.

A process whereby the entire colony was derogatorily portrayed through a wholesale feminization can also be noted. The colonizer's "masculinity" showed to the best advantage when contrasted/ compared with the ascribed "femininity" of the colonized. As Ashis Nandy points out,

> Colonization too was congruent with the existing Western stereotypes and the philosophy which they represented. It produced a cultural and social consensus in which political and socio-economic dominance symbolized the dominance of men and masculinity over women and femininity.[21]

As a perfect illustration of this, James Forbes describes Indian men as follows:

> In India, a people present themselves to our eyes, clothed in linen garments and somewhat low descending, of a garb and gesture we may say maidenly and well nigh effeminate, of a countenance shy and somewhat estranged, yet smiling out a glazed and somewhat bashful familiarity.[22]

"Shy," "bashful" and "maidenly," and also quite explicitly

"effeminate" – we can easily trace the progress of feminization here.

Rather ironically, female travel writers also resort to such feminization, reasserting the idea of inferiority associated with it. Eliza Fay refers to lack of physical strength in Indian men, who approximate female status when compared to "masculine" Englishmen. She quotes a Bengali servant: "Oh, I no English. I Bengalman. I no estrong like English; one, two, three Bengalman cannot do like one Englishman."[23] It seems quite possible that the "Bengalman" was using his weakness as an excuse, demonstrating what Homi Babha has called "canniness." But we need to place emphasis not just on what the Indian said, but also on the English woman's unquestioning acceptance of it. Obviously, there is a consensus among the colonizers that "Bengalmen" actually could not do what the Englishman did.

Despite this seeming uniformity in the feminization of India, we have to keep in mind that diverse effects of this were to be seen. While the male travellers could establish their superiority, no such easy reaction was open to the women. As collaborators in the colonial enterprize, they often had to submerge their own female identity and join in denouncing the very category of the feminine.

In one single area, the representation of women, and focussing basically on the binary category of male and female writers, several diverse trends could be traced within the colonial paradigm. This could be regarded as a signboard for other areas as well. We would be quite off track if we saw these diversities as somehow weakening aspects of the imperial edifice. Quite to the contrary, these co-existing diversities enabled the discourses of patriarchy and imperialism, Romanticism and rationalism – to mention only a few – to configure as non-contradictory for the practitioners. It is possible in postcolonial analysis to deploy these internal contradictions for unravelling purposes. But it has to be kept in mind at a prominent level that during the heyday of imperialism, these contradictions were precisely the aspects that contributed to the psychological coherence of the project.

Notes

A preliminary version of the few specific ideas in this essay relating to native-white women's relations was included in a paper entitled "Race or Gender?" which has been submitted for a forthcoming anthology edited by Ms Nirmala Nair.

1   Gayatri Chakravorty Spivak "Can the Subaltern Speak?", in Bill Ashcroft, Gareth Griffiths, Helen Tiffin, eds, *The Postcolonial Studies Reader*, (London: Routledge, 1995), 24-28.
2   Ashcroft, et al, *The Postcolonial Studies Reader*, 250.
3   As quoted in Kate Teltscher, *India Inscribed*, (Delhi: Oxford University Press, 1997), 8.
4   James Forbes, *Oriental Memoirs: Vols I-IV*, (New Delhi: Gian Publishing House, 1988).
5   Richard Burton, *Goa and the Blue Mountain*, (Delhi: Asian Educational Services, 1991) 107.
6   Ludovico de Varthema, *The Travels of Ludovico de Varthema*, (London: Hakluyt Society, 1863), 90.
7   John Huighen Van Linschoten, *Discourses of Voyages into the East and West Indies*, (London: Hakluyt Society, 1867), 209.
8   Ludovico de Varthema, *The Travels of Ludovico de Varthema*, 203.
9   Ludovico de Varthema, *The Travels of Ludovico de Varthema*, 135.
10   Isabella Fane, *Miss Fane in India*, (Gloucestershire: Allan Sattin, 1985), 48.
11   Peter Mundy, *The Travels of Peter Mundy in Asia and Europe*, (London: The Hakluyt Society, 1919), 42.
12   Kate Teltscher, *India Inscribed*, 45.
13   Gayatri Chakravorty Spivak, "Can the Subaltern Speak?", 295.
14   Thomas Twining, *Travels in India*, (London: Osgood, 1893), 465, original emphasis only on "seeing."
15   James Forbes, *Oriental Memoirs*, 321.
16   Kate Teltscher, *India Inscribed*, 51.
17   Emily Eden, *Up the Country*, (London: Oxford University Press, 1930), 309-310.
18   Eliza Fay, *Oriental Letters from India, 1779-1819*, (London: Hogarth Press, 1986), 203.

19   Eliza Fay, *Oriental Letters from India, 1779-1819*, 203.
20   Thomas Herbert, *A Relation of Some Yeares Travaile* 1638, (London: Hutton, 1938), 41.
21   Ashis Nandy, *The Intimate Enemy*, (Delhi: Oxford University Press, 1989), 4.
22   James Forbes, *Oriental Memoirs*, 55.
23   Eliza Fay, *Oriental Letters from India, 1779-1819*, 177-178.

References

1   Ashcroft, Bill, Gareth Griffiths, Helen Tiffin, eds, *The Postcolonial Studies Reader*, (London: Routledge, 1995).
2   Burton, Richard, *Goa and the Blue Mountain*, (Delhi: Asian Educational Services, 1991).
3   Eden, Emily, *Up the Country*, (London: Oxford University Press, 1930).
4   Fane, Isabella, *Miss Fane in India*, (Gloucestershire: Allan Sattin, 1985).
5   Fay, Eliza, *Oriental Letters from India, 1779-1819*, (London: Hogarth Press, 1986).
6   Forbes, James, *Oriental Memoirs* (4 volumes), (New Delhi: Gian Publishing House, 1988).
7   Herbert, Thomas, *A Relation of Some Yeares Travaile*, (London: Hutton, 1638).
8   Mundy, Peter, *The Travels of Peter Mundy in Asia and Europe*, (London: The Hakluyt Society, 1919).
9   Nandy, Ashis, *The Intimate Enemy*, (Delhi: Oxford University Press, 1989).
10   Spivak, Gayatri Chakravorty, "Can the Subaltern Speak?", in Ashcroft et al, 24-28, 1995.
11   Teltscher, Kate, *India Inscribed*, (Delhi: Oxford University Press, 1997).
12   Twining, Thomas, *Travels in India*, (London: Osgood, 1893).
13   Van Linschoten, John Huighen, *Discourses of Voyages into the East and West Indies*, (London: Hakluyt Society, 1867).
14   Varthema, Ludovico de, *The Travels of Ludovico de Varthema*, (London: Hakluyt Society, 1863).

TOURING AESTHETICS:
THE COLONIAL RHETORIC OF TRAVEL BROCHURES TODAY

PRAMOD K NAYAR

This paper explores the rhetoric of tourist brochures issued by departments of tourism run by the state or central government(s) in India.[1] It treats the brochures as a sub-genre of travel writing, and adopts a "literary" approach, locating certain figures of speech (tropes) in them. These figures of speech, I shall demonstrate, present a colonial image of the Indian landscape. While imperialism and colonialism were indisputably larger political "projects," my reading of tourist brochures explores the puzzling persistence of colonial rhetoric in post-Independence brochures. These brochures demonstrate extraordinary rhetorical similarity with the advertisements for the Empire Marketing Board, the P&O luxury cruises and Imperial Railways of the colonial period. I use the term "colonial" fully aware of the irony of its conjunction – in this essay – with underfinanced, poorly organized and frequently indifferent government-sponsored tourism.

Travel brochures, which constitute a major component of the

state government's publicity machine, are a peculiar genre. They are, on the one hand, straight-forward advertorials. On the other they are fantasy-like depictions of the state. They combine both the jingle of the advertisement and the rhetoric of government-sponsored programmes. In this essay my focus is on the rhetorical dimension of this amorphous genre. I assume here that travel brochures, like travel guides, are an integral constituent of travel/tourism and must be seen as travel-writing. They *write a travel* that is yet to take place.

Most tourist brochures are dominated by a "visualist ideology."[2] By this I mean that the tourist is directed, first and foremost, to *see*. While the experience of travel to and in a new place surely includes the entire ranges of senses, it is the visual element that is constantly emphasized in both the brochures and in the traveller's own attitude, which is characterized by the very commonplace statement, "seeing new places." This visualism may be discussed at two levels. One, the "aestheticization of the landscape" (a term used by Mary Louise Pratt) by casting it as a "scene" or a painting. Rivers and topographical features, fauna and flora and such are portrayed mostly as "pictures." I provide a brief list of commonly used terms that describe the landscape – scenery, kaleidoscope, sight, picturesque, breathtaking views, profiles, et cetera. The terms denote a freezing, in spatio-temporal terms, of the landscape (the word "scene" is, after all, derived from "skene," suggesting a tent or stage where a spectacle or event is to be presented and therefore perceived visually). These brochures describe and set out the scene of the natural landscape, the plant and animal life, the antiquities dotting the land, and the pleasures to be obtained from traversing this space/stage. The brochures undertake an aestheticization which is a carefully selected and ordered "version" of the landscape which describes the beauties and attractions alone. This aestheticization thus places the landscape into a frame, with well-defined boundaries. It therefore restricts the expanse, awesome size, or overwhelming topoi into something more controllable. Thus, the awe-inspiring, even frightening, hills, rivers, forests and wild beasts seem pleasant (because controlled) when thus viewed.

The second level is the status of the watcher. The tourist is the watcher who scans the landscape. The scanning confers a nearly panoptical power upon the watcher. S/he watches, controls, and interprets the passive, viewed landscape. This Foucauldian gaze inextricably links sight with power. As we shall see, this predication of viewer and viewed renders the landscape passive, to be conquered. I would like to suggest here that even if the tourist is a sympathetic, awe-struck viewer of the landscape, s/he is projected as a conqueror by the very act of seeing. Located within the site of a vehicle, a watchtower or within the safety of a group, the viewer casts himself or herself not only in the role of a viewer but also as the interpreter of what s/he sees. Thus, the viewing of a ruin is to participate in an awareness of history, of aesthetics, and the "human condition." The landscape, which lies ready to be interpreted is open to any kind of reading, depending upon the epistemological, ideological, political and cultural strategies and tools the viewer brings with her/him. The gaze is thus never an objective one, it is always interpretative. And interpretation is an act of power since it bestows a certain status upon the viewer/ interpreter. For instance, to read a ruin or landscape as "exotic" is to automatically summon up a range of ideas and ideologies of the irreducible otherness of the object, of the thrill of the new and strange, and of the incomprehensibility of the object (all elements of the exotic). The exotic is so precisely because of its difference from the familiar. To render a place "exotic" is to confer upon it the status and character of difference – an interpretative act of power.

While watching, the other senses may also be "indulged," even resulting in synaesthesia. Samples of this other-sensory rhetoric in brochures usually include the following – breathing in clean air, inhaling fragrances, hearing music of the tribal/rural musicians or women's anklets, or the taste of good food. Yet, in terms of sheer number, the visual images exceed any other-sensory ones. The visualization of the landscape leads to numerous "acts" on the tourist's part. Mystification, exoticization, conquest, acquisition, exploration and study, escape, dislocation, and affirmation of self-identity now occur. The exoticization of the landscape blends the bizarre, the strange with the familiar. Examples include – the car in the jungle, the forest vaguely familiar through repeated movie footage, the anticipated danger of the wild, and others. Terms used frequently to create this sense of strangeness include – mysterious, magical, exotic, new, unfold, undiscovered. Most brochures market the landscape of the tourist site under these exoticizing labels. Thus, a seduction through man's love for the strange and new is successfully "produced." The tourist is seduced into viewing the exotic. As I have already pointed out, the appeal of the exotic has to be achieved through an emphasis of difference. The tourist – or potential tourist – is drawn to the land with the attraction of seeing something different from the usual. Travel is primarily an exploration of the different and the new. The exoticization of the landscape in these brochures plays upon man's need for newness.

The mysterious landscape, having been viewed, must now be "explored." "Explore" is a favourite word in tourist brochures, occurring twice in a small Orissa Tourism handout, and thrice in one from Karnataka Tourism. The landscape transforms the tourist into a Cortez (one recalls Keats' Cortez who used his "eagle eyes" in "On First Looking into Chapman's Homer." Keats' poem is probably the finest "theoretical" study of a travel guide!) This exploration and "discovery" (of the landscape) is a premeditated surprise, a surprise anticipated on leaving home, "the ultimate kind of seizure by elsewhere."[3] One leaves home precisely to be surprised, or "awakened," as numerous brochures frequently describe the experience, before recommending the same.

Exploration and discovery is co-terminous with study. The landscape is (i) viewed from afar – as brochure pictures, guide books, or windows of cars (Bartkowski's "protected voyeurism"); (ii) approached, and therefore viewed from closer proximity; (iii) explored and studied carefully; (iv) interpreted, experienced and stored away as a restorative memory for future bad times when merely recalling the holiday acts as a stimulus.

The tourist studies the landscape's physical features, its particular-peculiar characteristics, and collects information of, say, rainfall, history, products, et cetera. S/he is thus voyeur-scientist-interpreter. Most tourist brochures thus offer glimpses "into" the tourist site in the form of brief introductory and informative descriptions. These usually include – exact location from nearest airport or railway station, height above sea level, the legend and history, topography, specific points of interest (and danger, as we shall see later), and so on. "Spectacular sunsets from the top of the hill," and the exact species of lions in the Gir Forest are two random samples I shall mention here. These descriptions form both the pretext and pre-text of the tourist's sighting/reading of the elsewhere. References to past glories, the local ruler's attitudes, the cultural richness are pretext-ual inspiration for the tourist to transform her/himself into scientist, seeker, interpreter.

The landscape is thus a subject to be studied. Yet, it is also a source of pleasure. The tourist is an Epicurean pleasure-seeker, even if it is the pleasure of knowledge. In such images, I find a startling profusion of Freudian "ingestion images," to coin a phrase. These images, as the phrase suggests, objectify the landscape as passive, *edible* things awaiting ingestion by the viewer. I list here a few such images frequently found in brochures – breathe in, savour, take in, imbibe, inhale. The landscape is thus internalized into the body of the tourist. This trope suggests a blurring of the subject-object predication. The tourist both surrenders to the seduction of the landscape, and takes the landscape into her/himself. The space/text of the land is recoded, and hence decoded by effacing its specificity. This de-scription is achieved through "ingestion" into the body/text of the tourist. The body of the tourist becomes a new topos where the landscape finds another ontology, or existence. This kind of "ontopology," to borrow a Derridean portmanteau term, with its psychoanalytic imagery, is itself extremely fascinating for the problematic of "identity" (man and land, man and animal, native and outsider-tourist). The studied, ingested landscape is also conquered in the course of exploration and seduction. Hills "waiting to be climbed," "caves asking to be explored," "flora and fauna waiting to be discovered" (actual descriptions in the brochures) are all tropes in the imperial/colonial mode.

Images of colonial "activity" are also simultaneous with the feminization of the landscape. The sexist, androcentric rhetoric abounds in images of a female, passive, prone landscape with the masculine, tourist-conquistador penetrating the interior. This imagery and rhetoric can provide interesting studies in reading the sexist rhetoric embedded in tourist brochures.

This "conquest" is also fraught with danger. Like colonial adventures of the past (and, no doubt, of the present, albeit in different "period costumes!"), the tourist heading into the landscape is also aware of impending danger. Brochures offer the danger of the unknown as a temptation. Adventure tourism is a major industry today. The traveller's seduction occurs by the offer of both awe and wonder, beauty and terror. The brochures offer a new, strange world wherein the tourist faces danger and benefits from it.

Here, two parallels are striking. One, of the genre of adventure fiction that entices the would-be colonial with "dreams of adventure" into committing "deeds of empire," to borrow Martin Green's famous phrase. Two, the Wordsworthian sublime of awe and wonder closely parallels the fetish and phobia exhibited by the Westerner towards the natives (Homi K Bhabha's formulation). The parallels, I argue, must be noted since adventure fiction and Western approaches to the natives seem to share a similar colonial rhetoric with tourist brochures. Here, the tourist is both awed and attracted by the new land, topography, and native. Paradoxically, it is this awareness of danger that seduces the tourist into leaving the safety of her/his home.

This "dangerous" other world is the one we ought to seek. Thus, the brochures suggest a "leaving behind" (a pet phrase in such brochures) of the "mundane" for the "extraordinary" (also a frequently used descriptive) Other. The tourist is turned into a near-fugitive, seeking to escape. The Other world offers opportunities – and we shall examine the notion of choices so often advertized – that this world does not. These are opportunities valued for their rarity – of danger, great natural beauty, strange sights, and in today's high pollution environment, "clean" air. Once again, I draw a parallel here with the early British arrivals in the East. These were Englishmen who saw the East as a chance to escape boredom, failure and poverty in England. India and the East offered an opportunity to secure wealth and adventure, prestige and identity. The tourist is thus such a "seeker" too, like the Western adventurers of yore.

The opportunities offered are those of appropriation and acquisition. Various types of this acquisition pattern may be sketched –

(i) Acquiring rare bargains, through shopping. The tourist is a businessman who seeks pleasure and pays for the same, while always seeking a good deal. The brochures frequently suggest that the pleasures accrued from travel and, of course, spending time in the marketplace, are worth more than what the tourist actually pays;

(ii)   Museum/art centre tourism, which makes the tourist a "cultural traveller";

(iii) Acquisition of knowledge, where the tourist purchases photographs, indigenous products, histories to gain information about a new place/culture;

(iv)   In recent times, tourist brochures advocate travel to acquire health. The hotels and holiday homes advertized, if of an elite, expensive class, frequently provide gymnasia, swimming, yoga, meditation, and health spa facilities to the tourist. Travel, which removes the individual from his usual stress-inducing environment, thus provides a new lease of life;

(v)   Travel as a means of self-discovery. The tourist who takes decisions, "roughing it" in the woods, partakes of a new "community" (fellow travellers) or embraces solitude temporarily, and discovers her/himself. Thus, the acquisition of a sense of self-identity, and of one's own native, regional and cultural difference (from the Other) results from travel.

One therefore acquires a sense of identity and cultural heritage, knowledge, health and wealth. Cultural travel is a major component of tourist brochures. The acquisition of culture – itself reflective of the Western ideology of acquisition, as James Clifford (1988) has demonstrated – occurs through the individual's transplantation into a "contact zone." "Contact zones," as Mary Louise Pratt defines them, are "social spaces where disparate cultures meet, clash and grapple with each other, often in highly asymmetrical relations of domination and subordination."[4] A "transculturation" occurs in this contact zone. Brochures advertise museums, art centres and ethnic-indigenous handicraft "villages" where objects and artefacts of another culture may be acquired. The tourist-businessman (even the "family-tourist," travelling with the entire family) purchases relics,

or such ethnic cultural objects, and learns about them in such
contact zones. However, the relationship is more of trade here, and
less violent than Pratt suggests. The monetization of culture, its
packaging and marketing, modify relations into economic terms –
tourist as buyer, native as seller.

A certain erasure or segregation of native cultures at certain
specific places of the tourist visit may also occur. The creation of
handicraft villages, transplanted "cultural markets" and exhibitions
produce a dislocation of the native from her/his land. This parallel
"travel" of displacement is an interesting phenomenon attributable
at least partly to tourism. This segregatory tendency of
contemporary tourism is an exoticization and a circumscription.
The native culture separated from its point of origin has an exotic
flavour for two reasons. (i) The difference from the rest of the
tourist's itinerary is underlined in these "pockets." (ii) Separated
from the original "setting" creates an aura of mystery around the
cultural artefact or artisan as Susan Stewart has argued in *On
Longing.*[5] It limits the intrusion of the native culture by transplanting
it into more controlled surroundings, and thereby is "organized"
native culture. The tourist, passing through such organized native
sites gets a synoptic view of indigenous cultures without actual
immersion in them.

A certain "mass discovery of the countryside" occurs, especially
with the increasing mobility of the tourist.[6] The native cultural
"zone" is transformed into a contact zone of/for discovery by the
tourist seeker. The contemporary traveller does not, evidently,
exhibit the colonial justifications for travel – imperial knowledge-
gathering or exploitation of resources, to mention just two. The
contact zone here is the result of several political and cultural
factors, such as migration. The intensity of interaction within the
contact zone is also different in degree from the colonial period.
The duration of the contact, the monetary transactions, the

emphasis on pleasure are all factors that distinguish contemporary travel from colonial travel. I would, however, like to suggest that the exoticization of native cultures in the form of tourist exhibition sites, for instance, reinstates the asymmetrical nature of contact zone interaction that Pratt describes. The purchasing power of the tourist-consumer, the museological mode of exhibiting cultures, and the state's active intervention in the actual "presentation" of itself within the brochures are all locutions of power in the social space of tourism.

This "contact zone" need not only be at the "cultural" level, as Pratt suggests. One can see a transculturation in the emphasis on a shift to "nature," advocated by most tourist brochures. These brochures suggest a return to the wilds that is supposedly a different "culture." One leaves the safety of the home, car, city for the "wild expanses," as the Uttar Pradesh Tourism brochure describes it. They tempt the tourist with a pre-civilized world where one can be "true." The Orissa Tourism brochure actually uses the word "uncage," a literal and metaphoric representation of the movement from home-culture-artificial to the outside-natural-true. Once more, the nature/culture division is emphasized.

If tourism is a return to the wilds, it is also a pilgrimage to the past. It is a paradoxical feature of the brochures that, on the one hand, they recommend a return to the jungle, and on the other, suggest a crusade-like return to one's cultural roots. Travel for cultural aims, as mentioned above, to acquire a heritage. Most brochures hence specify ancient glories, especially wealth, ethnic art (the repeatedly advertized "handmade"), and indigenous traditions. A certain pan-national movement is recommended, if one goes by the brochures. This is to facilitate greater knowledge of our country and an acquisition of pride in its heritage.[7]

And finally, a brief look at the packaging of pleasure and desire in these brochures. The tourist is today projected more as consumer than producer. From a producer in this world, last of an assembly line of many such, s/he becomes a purveyor-connoisseur-consumer on these travels. This consumer role has numerous facets, all associated with travel. I shall quickly mention a few, since a detailed analysis is not within the scope of this paper.

Tourism is a question of style today. It has a certain "sign value" in its consumption. The need for touring/relaxation is constructed when the brochures create new types of perceived use values, or what Jean Baudrillard (1985) terms "sign value." The commodity-object may be culture, history, health and all the acquisitive possibilities discussed above. Far more than exchange or use, the tourist consumer (now reduced to an appendage to the commodity-object exactly when, paradoxically, s/he is advertized as "Maharajah" by the advertisers) involves in "a sacrificial logic of consumption, gift, expenditure, potlatch." Thus, the images-meanings overlap, and stylization of the tourist consumer occurs in the course of her/his travels and acquisition (through the "culture industry?" Perhaps.)

The question of clientele is also relevant here. Tourism's targets range across age, gender and class. Variation in the "elite tourism" rhetoric occurs to suit, say, the upper class clientele who can afford "star hotel" luxuries. Economy tourism frequently advertises its prices, while the first type almost never does. The packaging of the culture at the contact zone is also obviously different to cater to the changed clientele.

The rhetoric of tourist brochures thus market aesthetics, culture, health, and creates a certain "acquisitiveness" in the traveller. The parallels with colonial rhetoric, the tropes, and the marketing of sign values are all integral to these brochures. Surely, the brochures are as literary as travel memoirs and fiction? An interesting comparison may be found in *The Oxford Book of Travel Verse*. From lesser known figures like Thomas Hood to celebrities like Coleridge, poets have used similar rhetoric in their travel poems. In the above collection, nearly 85-90% of the verse is filled with images of acquisition, the dual emotions of awe and wonder, ingestion, adventure, conquest and others that we located in tourist brochures.

The tourist brochures create both a "shikari" (hunter) and an aesthete in its tourist. One might even say that aesthetics has really travelled far today. The continuing persistence of colonial rhetoric in government issued tourist brochures is an interesting phenomenon. Perhaps the colonialism over the land has changed in terms of the nature of colonials but not in the approaches. A study of this rhetoric should, I can speculate, be incorporated into a study of the sociology of leisure and recreation in contemporary India.

Notes

1   Some clarification and elaboration is in order here. I have made use of brochures issued by the Departments of Tourism from the following states – Orissa, Uttar Pradesh, Andhra Pradesh, Kerala and Karnataka. The argument is "distilled" from these samples. Variations exist, and in a few cases, contradict my study. However, the overall veracity of this set of arguments stands. Occasionally, advertisements in newspapers and magazines have also been used. Admittedly, the purposes of travel are different today. The white traveller in India frequently had an imperial purpose – gathering knowledge about the East for a Western audience. Here tourism served the purpose of appropriation, as seen in travelogues right from Edward Terry and John Ovington in the seventeenth century. Then there were travellers such as Fanny Parkes who sought the exotic and the picturesque curiosities of the Orient. While a hierarchy of travellers and travel-writing – and their corresponding differentiated mechanisms of appropriation – is perhaps in order here, my reading is based on the assumption that the encoding of colonial themes in contemporary tourist brochures suggests the persistence of the appropriative tendency of tourism in general. A fuller study of these brochures requires the explication of several other issues and themes. Some of them are: the role of multinational corporations and business houses in

123

tourism, the marketing of ethnicity in tourism, the exoticization of native/ indigenous populations, the actual composition of travellers (their class backgrounds, for instance), and finally, the ecological impact of travel. All of these, I suggest, would constitute a study of the sociology of leisure in contemporary India. These are, however, excluded from the ambit of the present essay, which focusses only on the rhetorical features of contemporary tourist brochures.

2   Mary Louise Pratt's reading of imperial travel analyzes the rhetoric of the visual. Pratt argues that a relation of *mastery* predicated between the seer and the seen inform imperial travel narratives. Pratt, describing such a traveller writes: "what Burton sees is all there is, and that the landscape was intended to be viewed from where he has emerged upon it." Mary Louise Pratt, *Imperial Eyes: Travel Writing and Transculturation*, (New York: Routledge, 1992), 204-5.

3   Frances Bartkowski, *Travellers, Immigrants, Inmates: Studies in Estrangement*, (Minneapolis: University of Minnesota Press, 1995), 21-34.

4   Mary Louise Pratt, *Imperial Eyes*, 4.

5   Susan Stewart, *On Longing: Narratives of the Miniature, the Gigantic, the Souvenir, the Collection*, (Durham and London: Duke University Press, 1993).

6   For a discussion of this theme, especially with regard to rural England in the early part of this century, see Alan Tomlinson and Helen Walker, "Holidays for All: Popular Movements, Collective Leisure and the Pleasure Industry," in Alan Tomlinson, ed, *Consumption, Identity and Style: Marketing, Meanings and the Packaging of Pleasure*, (London and New York: Routledge, 1990).

7   It might be interesting to study the rhetoric of these brochures with their pan-Indian and simultaneously firmly "local" recommendations in connection with the nationalist discourses of contemporary India.

References

1   Bartkowski, Frances, *Travellers, Immigrants, Inmates: Studies in Estrangement*, (Minneapolis: University of Minnesota Press, 1995).

2   Baudrillard, Jean, "The Ecstasy of Communication," in Hal Foster, ed, *Postmodern Culture*, (London: Pluto, 1985).

3   Clifford, James, *The Predicament of Culture: Twentieth Century Ethnography, Literature and Art*, (Cambridge, Massachusetts: Harvard University Press, 1988).

4   Crossley-Holland, Kevin, ed, *The Oxford Book of Travel Verse*, (Oxford: Clarendon Press, 1986).

5   Foster, Hal, ed, *Postmodern Culture*, (London: Pluto, 1985).

6   Keats, John, "On First Looking into Chapman's Homer," *Poetical Works*, Edited by H W Garrod, (London: Oxford University Press, 1976).

7 Pratt, Mary Louise, *Imperial Eyes: Travel Writing and Transculturation*, (New York: Routledge, 1992).

8 Stewart, Susan, *On Longing: Narratives of the Miniature, the Gigantic, the Souvenir, the Collection*, (Durham and London: Duke University Press, 1993).

9 Tomlinson, Alan, ed, *Consumption, Identity and Style: Marketing, Meanings and the Packaging of Pleasure*, (London and New York: Routledge, 1990).

10 Tomlinson, Alan, and Walker, Helen, "Holidays for All: Popular Movements, Collective Leisure and the Pleasure Industry," in Tomlinson, 1990.

EMPIRE WRITES BACK?
KANNADA TRAVEL FICTION AND NATIONALIST DISCOURSE

V B THARAKESHWAR

In this essay I attempt to explore the process of the formation of a nationalist identity through travel as witnessed in the Kannada travelogues and fiction where travel is a major component of the narrative. In the first section, placing them in the context of colonialism and nationalism in India, I try to explain how translation and travel play a major role in constructing new subjectivities. This leads us to the question of the construction of the "self" and the "other" during the colonial cultural transactions. In the second section, I look at some Kannada travel writings to see how the nationalist "self" and its "other" get constructed in it. In the third section, I look at the formation of a Kannada nationalist identity, not in terms of a pan-nationalist framework, but through more localized concerns to locate how the Kannada nationalist "self" defines itself by constructing non-colonial "others." I also argue for looking at Kannada travel writings emerging from journeys other than to the West.

I

Travel writing is a major genre in the Orientalist discourse, where
Western anthropologists, historians, sociologists and administrators
of colonial India who travelled to the colonies have "written down"
the native culture to produce an Orientalist discourse.[1] They
translated native culture in such a way as to recast it as an "other"
which in turn would help them in constructing their own "self." Said,
in *Orientalism*, exposes powerfully the complicity of the colonial
discourse with colonial rule and the nexus between knowledge and
power.[2] Travel writings that are part of the Orientalist discourse
participate in the production of "self" and "other" by translating
existing power relations between the colonizer and the colonized into
discourse, and also sustain them by reproducing itself.

There are several studies on travel writing that are part of the
colonial/orientalist discourse. The relation between translation, travel
and intercultural contacts have been already highlighted by several
studies such as *Imperial Eyes: Travel Writing and Transculturation* (1992)
by Mary Louise Pratt, and the relationship between colonialism and
colonial travel writing in *Women Travellers in Colonial India: The Power of
the Female Gaze* (1998) by Indira Ghose. Similarly several studies
also focus on the mobile theorists and how the location of it affects
their theory such as *Traveling Theories, Traveling Theorists* (1989), edited
by James Clifford and Vivek Dhareshwar, "The Third World
Academic in Other Places; or, the Postcolonial Intellectual Revisited"
(1997) by Rajeshwari Sundar Rajan and "The Postcolonial Aura:
Third World Criticism in the Age of Global Capitalism" (1994) by
Arif Dirlik. But there are only a few studies that focus on the
nationalist discourse, or travel writings that form part of such a
discourse such as: a study of the reversal of the gaze by Indian
travellers to England can be found in "Making Spectacle of Empire:
Indian Travellers in Fin-de-Siecle London"(1996) by Antoinette
Burton. Looking at the travelogue in Kannada as well as at a text in

which travel is a major component of the narrative, this paper is an attempt at analyzing the construction of a national identity through the description of the experience of travel, both real and fictionalized.

Before going into the particularities of the travelogue in Kannada, I briefly sum up some of the features of the nationalist discourse. One of the pioneering studies in this area is Partha Chatterjee's *Nationalist thought and Colonial World: A Derivative Discourse?* (1986). Chatterjee studies cultural nationalism and traces the development of nationalist thought in India. He says that there is a seeming contradiction in Indian nationalism. According to him nationalism "produced a discourse in which even as it challenged the colonial claim to political domination, it also accepted the very intellectual premise of "modernity" on which colonial domination was based"[3] He employs the categories "thematic" and "problematic" to explain this seeming contradiction in nationalist thought. He tries to separate the claims of an ideology, i.e., its identification of historical possibilities and the practical or programmatic forms of its realization, from its justificatory structures, i.e., the nature of the evidence it presents in support of those claims, the rules of inference it relies on to logically relate a statement of the evidence to a structure of arguments, the set of epistemological principles, and finally the set of ethical principles it appeals to in order to assert that those claims are morally justified.

He calls the former part as the problematic and the latter part its thematic.

The thematic, in other words, refers to an epistemological as well as ethical system which provides a framework of elements and rules for establishing relations between elements; the problematic, on the other hand, consists of concrete statements about possibilities justified by reference to the thematic.

His contention is that the problematic in nationalist thought is exactly the reverse of that of Orientalism. That is to say, the "object" in nationalist thought is still the Oriental, who retains the essentialist character depicted in Orientalist discourse. Only he is not passive, non-participating. He is seen to possess a "subjectivity" which he can himself "make." In other words, while his relationship to himself and to others is "posed, understood and defined" by others, i.e., by an objective scientific consciousness, by Knowledge, by Reason, those relationships are not acted by others. His subjectivity, he thinks, is active, autonomous and sovereign.[4]

Chatterjee is trying to show that at the level of thematic the nationalist thought is adopting the same essentialist conceptions of "the East" and "the West," the "typology created by a transcendent studying subject, and hence the same 'objectifying' procedures of knowledge constructed in the post-Enlightenment age of western science." His central concern is to explore the "relation between the content of nationalist discourse and the kind of politics which nationalism conducts." He says that

> It is part of the ideological content of nationalism, which takes as its adversary a contrary discourse – the discourse of colonialism. Pitting itself against the reality of colonial rule – which appears before it as an existent, almost palpable, historical truth – nationalism seeks to assert the feasibility of entirely political possibilities. These are its political claims which colonialist discourse haughtily denies.[5]

Thus both colonial discourse and the national discourse share a similar epistemology of the post-Enlightenment world (the thematic), but the arguments, which are derived from it, are different, as the politics of both the discourses are different. One seeks to produce a problematic that justifies its colonial rule; the other produces a problematic that questions the colonial rule. Further Chatterjee tells us that the relation between nationalist discourse and the forms of modern Western thought is not a simple relation

129

of correspondence, or even of derivation. First of all, nationalist thought is selective about what it takes from Western thought. He asserts that it is indeed deliberately and necessarily selective, as its politics is to oppose the colonial rule and reject the immediate political implications of colonial thought so that it can argue in favour of political possibilities which colonialist thought refuses to admit. Chatterjee's hypothesis is that a nationalist discourse is "a different discourse, yet one that is dominated by another (colonial discourse)."

In a metaphorical way I call this a translation of colonial discourse into nationalist discourse by the upper caste English educated elite of the colonial period, where the translated discourse appears to be similar but also different from the colonial discourse as the knowledge and power relationship it seeks to establish is different from the latter.[6] Here translation points to the role of the upper caste English educated elite in translating the colonial discourse into a nationalist discourse to produce a subjectivity called Nationalist. In this process of translation of colonial discourse into nationalist discourse the subjectivity of the upper caste English educated elite gets transformed (translated) into a nationalist elite, i.e., the translator gets translated in the process of translation.[7]

Another crucial point made by Chatterjee concerns the division by nationalist discourse of culture into spiritual and material domains, to challenge the claims of superiority by the colonial culture. Such a division enabled Indian nationalists to claim that the East was superior to the West in the spiritual domain, though the West may be superior in the material. This material/spiritual dichotomy was further carried to another form – the outer and the inner, which applied to the matter of concrete day-to-day living in terms of home and the world. For the nationalists, the home, with its representative being the woman, was to remain uncontaminated by the profanity of the material world.

The "woman question" was a central issue during the early part of cultural nationalism. To reframe it, in Sangari and Vaid's words, Woman was a site on which the opposition to colonialism was carried out by the nationalist elite during the colonial period.[8] One must read the Kannada travel writings in the background of these frames in order to comprehend how a nationalist self gets constructed using woman as a site, excluding the non-upper castes from this nationalist construction of the self.

Travel writing of the nationalist ilk is anti-colonial, though it is not anti-modernity; it accepts the superiority of the West in the material domain, and tries to achieve it by modernizing itself or appropriating it and claiming it as its own. An analysis of the travel writings on England by Indian writers reveals this phenomenon. Antoinette Burton shows how these travel writings try to write back to the Empire, using the City of London as a site to do so.[9] Providing historical evidence of how imperial power could be interrogated by "natives" in the "mother city of the kingdom and the Empire" itself, she narrates how the native traveller did not simply return the gaze,

> but demonstrated how readily available its disciplinary regimes were for contest and refiguration – especially by Indian men, whose pretensions to nationhood and its cultural corollary, Victorian masculinity, were under scrutiny at this particular historical juncture."[10]

My own study henceforth evinces and extends Burton's thesis as it looks at the colony writing back to the master to empower itself and to claim a kind of collective identity, and probes the nature of the nationalist self formed at the crossroads of upper caste and male identities. I also argue at the end for interrogating nationalist discourse not in the binary frame of colonial/national but in a more complex matrix of self and other by looking at travel writing to places other than the West.

II

The genre of travel writing as it exists today is itself a new genre in the Kannada literary tradition. It is an instance of appropriation/translation of a genre from the colonizer's culture by the colonized culture to match up to the culture of the colonizer and fill a lacuna that it perceives when it sees itself in the eyes of an Orientalist. In that sense Kannada travel writing has been appropriated from the Empire, and deployed to construct a self that is anti-colonial and yet modern.

Though many had travelled out of Karnataka in the nineteenth century itself, we hardly find anyone writing about it. Till the 1960s, it is England and other European nations that attracted more Kannadigas towards it. In princely Mysore both the King Krishnaraja Odeyar and the Diwan, Vishweswaraia had travelled extensively in England and Europe. These travels had helped them to build princely India as a model state in India. As a consequence of their visit, we find them taking up many developmental activities in princely Mysore, including state-driven industrialization and a move towards democratization of administrative structures. Shivaram Karanth's *Apoorva Paschima* (Unique Europe), Dinakar Desai's *Na Kanda Paduvana* (The West I Saw), Karaveera Andaneppa Kulakarni's *Europe Kandada Pravasa* (Travel to European Continent) in 1929, Ra Si's *Koravanjiya Paduvan Yatre* (Koravanji's Travel to West), Gokak's *Samudradacheyinda* (From the Other Side of the Sea) are some of the travelogues that show that it is Europe and England that beckoned Kannadigas. In the postcolonial period we witness a shift towards America from Europe. Some of these travelogues are B G L Swamy's *Amerikadalli Naanu* (Me in America), Dr Krishnanada Kamat's *Naanu Americage Hogidde* (Even I had Gone to America), Gorur Ramaswamy Iyengar's *Americadalli Goruru* (Goruru in America), A N Moorty Rao's *Apara Vayaskana America Yaatre* (The Tour of an Old man in America), Prabhushankar's *Americadalli Naanu, Shanti* (Me and Shanti in

America), Nadig Krishnamurhty's *Saagaradaache* (Beyond the Sea)
et cetera. However, from the 1950s, Russia appears more
consistently in travel writings, since many of those who travelled
were famous writers such as De Javaregowda's *Videshadalli Naalku
Vaara* (Four Weeks in a Foreign Land), Sriranga Raju's *Soviet Dinachari*
(Soviet Dairy), Biligiri Ramachandra Raya's *Naanu Kanda Russia* (The
Russia I Saw), Basavaraja Kattimani's *Naanu Kanda Russia* (The Russia
I Saw), G S Shivarudrappa's *Mascowdalli Ippatteradu Dina* (Twenty
Two days in Moscow) et cetera. Thus in the colonial era, it was
England and other European countries that attracted Kannadigas,
in the post-colonial era it is America and Russia, though in terms of
numbers, it is certainly America now that dominates the scene (based
on the survey done by Vidyashankar, 1991).

The focus of this paper, however, is mainly on Kannada travel
writings on England, from the nineteenth century to the middle of
the twentieth, which I eventually link up with the formation of a
pan-Indian nationalist identity and also a Kannada nationalist identity,
to point out the double national identities that were present in the
Kannada context of the time.

The first translation from English to Kannada that can be considered
a travel narrative is John Bunyan's *Pilgrim's Progress*, translated by
G Wiegle in 1847. The first novel translated from English into Kannada
by Krishnaswamy Iyengar is *Robinson Crusoe*. We do not have sufficient
data to analyze the reception of these translations during that period.
We can safely argue that in this sense, travel and colonialism through
translation mark the birth of modern Kannada literature. Though
people went to England and other places from Karnataka in the
nineteenth century itself, we had to wait till 1936 to get a full-fledged
travel writing in the form of a diary. V K Gokak, a well known scholar
and a Gyanpeeth award winner, gives us travel writing in the form of
a diary written during his stay in London, where he had gone for
higher education. It is titled *Samudradaacheyinda* (From the Other Side

of the Ocean). But as a theme, travelling to England appears in Kannada novels much earlier.

There are references to crossing the ocean and to its consequences on our society, which broaden into a discussion on the consequences of modernity. The writers believe that crossing the ocean is prohibited for a Hindu. Thus, the first Kannada social novel, *Indira Bayi*, written by a Saraswat Brahmin called Gulvadi Venkat Rao, has a detailed discussion of travelling to England and its consequences. This novel is part of social reform novels that sprang up around this period in various languages of India at the turn of the nineteenth century.[11]

The narrative revolves around Bhaskara Raya, a young Saraswat Brahmin, who has finished his BA examination with distinction. He has been awarded a scholarship by the Government of India to go to England to do his CS. He takes this news to Kamalapura when he visits his mother and his guardian, sponsoring his studies. When he breaks the news to his mother, she is worried because crossing the ocean goes against their religion. She is also worried that in foreign countries he may have to eat food cooked by Mlecchas (outsiders, or non-Hindus; even non-Brahmins come under this category). To that, Bhaskara Raya assures her that Amrita Raya, his guardian, is willing to send a Brahmin cook with him to England. His mother is also worried about the availability of water uncontaminated by the touch of mlecchas. To this Bhaskara Raya's response is: "Where is the water which is not touched by the mlecchas? The Brahmins never dig the well, it is only others who dig the well and Brahmins use that water." When his mother says, "What if they touch it? And how can we clean it by putting in shuddodhaka (cow dung)," Bhaskara Raya replies, "OK. Let me carry a glass of shuddodhaka from here to London." She then warns him that the elders of the community would throw him out of the caste if he went to England. Bhaskara Raya assures her again by saying that they would not resort to banishment, as more and more people would be going to England, and if they throw all of them out of the caste, no one would be left in that caste.[12]

In the above discussion between Bhaskara Raya and his mother we see how pragmatism, traditional belief and reason work together. Bhaskara's mother is worried about the consequences of travel across sea and the non-availability of the food cooked by a Brahmin in the journey. A Brahmin cook has to be sent to overcome this hurdle. Then she is also worried about the water, which should not be contaminated by the mleccha. Then Bhaskara employs reason to convince her that no water is clean, because the well is itself dug by non-Brahmins. So there is no point in worrying about the "contaminated" water. Again a pragmatic solution crops up, that of carrying shuddodhaka, sprinkling a few drops of which on polluted things/food would make it usable for a Brahmin. It is not only a modern rationale and pragmatic that is deployed here to negotiate the challenges that modernity has put before Bhaskara. It is not just the story of Bhaskara but also the plight of the English educated upper caste in general. Bhaskara is not alone in his negotiations with modernity and tradition.

Before going to London, Bhaskara Raya invites all the graduates of Kamalapura to dinner. After dinner, they start discussing the sea voyage of Bhaskara Raya and its consequences. They talk about the social ostracism and boycotting that the caste institution like Mattas might impose on him. They also talk about how these things will help in speeding up the reforms in Hindu religion. To take up proper measures in this regard, they plan to meet at Jubilee Town Hall on the coming Sunday. Thus it is a collective fight that the English educated upper caste wages over the non-English educated "traditional" upper caste people and institutions. The lure of material wealth and prestige offered by English education and the trip to England is on the one hand, and the non-material benefits on the other. It would be interesting to ask why the upper caste institutions are against sea voyage. They are so deeply immersed in the discourse of modernity and rationality that they are also worried about the speed of social reforms in Hindu religion and society (read upper caste), and hence the anxiety about the smallest hint of transformation. The answer could be found in the latter part of the novel when Bhaskara returns from England.

After coming back from England, Bhaskara Raya marries a widow, Indirabai, from whose name the novel takes its title. The caste institution excommunicates the family members who were involved in this blasphemous marriage and others who supported it get partial excommunication. This points out to the fact that if a journey to a far off land is taken up, then new ideas enter into "our" culture and it will disturb the "equilibrium" (read hierarchy) that "our" culture has achieved. The potentiality of the journey is to bring in new ideas to push culture and the power relations that sustain it to a new "equilibrium" of those power relations. Here modernity, the journey to England, social reform in Hinduism, get linked with each other. Though English education is considered responsible for modern reasoning and a critique of "tradition" in the novel, the tension between "tradition" and "modernity" gets played out in the context of a journey. Thus women (albeit an upper caste woman) becomes the site to foreground the point of intersection of two different cultures.

However, at the end of the novel, there is an indication that more and more people have gone to England and returned home, and that the caste institution itself has adapted to the changing circumstances by coming up with rituals to purify the foreign-returned Brahmins in order to accept them again into the caste fold. Thus, in the first Kannada social novel itself, a journey to England is linked with modernity. It shows how a caste identity gets modernized through travel in order to face the challenges posed by the colonial culture and the question of women becomes prominent in such an intercultural encounter.

At this point, let me bring in Sir M Vishweswaraiah, who is considered to be the architect of modern Mysore. Sir M Vishweswaraiah was the Diwan of Mysore in the early part of the twentieth century and resigned from his post, protesting against the decision of the king to implement the Miller's Committee Report, which had recommended reservation of jobs for backward classes in administration. He represents the moment of arrival of nationalism and modernization of the nation in the history of nationalism in Karnataka. He established many industries in princely Mysore and was the brain behind constructing a dam across the river Cauvery. He also established many public institutions in princely Mysore. He had the dream of making princely Mysore a modern state. He wanted the Mysore state to have a port of its own for export and import, and so he requested the Madras presidency to allocate some land for it along the western coast. But the colonial state, after the fall of Tipu Sultan, while returning the conquered territory to the Odeyar dynasty, kept the coastal region in its hands, ensuring that Mysore would not develop into an independent state by denying the same to them.

Sir M Vishweswaraiah also played a major role in establishing the Kannada Sahitya Parishat, to develop modern literature in Kannada. He had travelled extensively to Japan, Italy, England, America, Canada, Sweden and Russia. Raja Seva Prasakta Sri M G Rangaiah recalls that then, for many youngsters of Mysore, Sir M Vishweswaraiah was a model to be emulated. In Sir M Vishweswaraiah's opinion, education in England and travels to other countries broadened the perspective of the people and made them progressive.[13] As he had travelled extensively to many European countries, he had seen many countries that were smaller than Mysore but scientifically advanced and modern. He wanted to develop princely Mysore into a modern nation with scientific advancement and industrialization. Raja Sevasakta

Sri D C Subbarayappa recollects an incident in this regard – Sir M Vishweswaraiah advising His Highness the Maharaja of Mysore to go on a trip to Western countries which would help in planning the progress of the province, and encouraging him to send the Prince of the Mysore province for such trips.[14]

Thus, travel to the West is perceived as a major means of modernizing the province of the East. Sir M Vishweswaraiah has written about the planned development of a nation through five year plans in the 1920s itself, that is much before Nehru implemented the same for the sovereign Indian nation-state later in the 1950s, and almost around the same time as it was implemented by Stalin in erstwhile USSR. The first Diwan of Mysore, Sri Rangacharlu, was of the opinion that it was essential to borrow new elements from another culture to modernize the country. He encouraged his subordinates to undertake foreign trips, and when they came back, offered them good positions in the State administration.[15] He himself had faced restrictions from his caste when he undertook a sea voyage from Madras to Calcutta, though he never cared for those restrictions.[16] Thus under the leadership of the benevolent King and Diwans who were for democratization of the state and for industrial development of the province Mysore made big strides and their action and thinking influenced the people of Mysore. The above description of Diwan Rangacharlu is by D V Gundappa, who is a well-known litterateur in Kannada and who also actively took part in the politics of the day. His was a prominent voice in the public sphere of princely Mysore during the first half of the twentieth century when he became one of the earliest to speak for a responsible government in Mysore.

Nationalist discourse perceived a kind of lacuna in the Indian culture, in its being "traditional" and not yet "modern," and tried to fill it up/appropriate it through opening its doors to new ideas. The new ideas came either through travel to European countries or through translations directly from English or via translations from Bangla and Marathi. But interestingly, in all these cultural transactions the question of women's position becomes important. In other words, women become the site on which these transactions take place. As discussed earlier, *Indira Bayi*, the first Kannada social novel deals with a widow's remarriage. Bhaskara Raya who comes back from England marries a widow. This question gets repeated in other social novels like Kerooru Vasudevacharya's *Indira* (1908) and Bolara Baburaya's *Vagdevi* (1905). The nationalists, as Chatterjee says, were interested only in redefining the notion of woman so that she can be under new patriarchy that was coming up in the context of modernity. Social reform was a means through which they tried to redefine women. They resolved the question of women by making a distinction between material and spiritual aspects of culture and through associations made women the custodian of protecting the "spiritual" aspect of Indian culture as they were eager to catch up with the technological aspect of modernity to outdo the colonial master. This aspect of the nationalist discourse, that of making women the custodians of Indian culture becomes clearer when we look at the first full-fledged travelogue in Kannada.

Samudradaacheyinda is a travelogue in the form of a diary, written by V K Gokak during his sojourn to England for higher studies, where he stayed for nearly two years. The cultural encounter with the West begins and gets a sharp rejection as soon as Gokak, or broadly speaking, the upper caste, middle class, English-educated, gets onto the ship. The upper caste, upper/middle class men are astonished to see a white woman travelling alone. They are shocked and scandalized seeing Western women and the way they dress on the deck, and dub their costume "obscene" and "vulgar," bringing in the rhetoric of "we" and "them" to explain these differences. Indian women who don such clothes are dubbed as Westernized. On reaching England, thus, women become the convenient site on which native men construct categories of "us" and "them."

On the third day of his journey on the ship, Gokak writes:

> The behaviour of English women on the ship draws our attention. [Following men] these women are ready to travel even to the North Pole. They can swim, jump, laugh, smoke like men. Sometimes they dress like men, too! This is not civilization. "The Empire" has created this new model.[17]

For Gokak, to know that women can do all that men can is shocking. The erosion of gender differences is not a matter of celebration, but something that has to be denounced. He unhesitatingly states that the erosion of gender differences is not natural to his part of civilization, but a new model created by the Empire. Here, the Western woman, who dresses like men and does all that they can do, gets represented as the Empire that has to be condemned.

Gokak condemns the English tradition, in which both men and women dance together. He says, "I don't know whether it is good for them or not, but I am sure that it is not good for our people."[18] In another incident, in a party thrown by a boy who has passed the examination to the Indian Civil Services, a Hindu woman dances. Gokak comments, "[T]here is no need to express *our* happiness by dancing like *them*."[19] At one point, Gokak recounts a debate at Oxford union over the motion that the House would support a measure under which a separation – whether voluntary or judicial – should mature into divorce at the end of three years on the petition of either spouse. In the course of this debate, a woman addresses the President as "Madam President," because male members of the union invited to the Ladies' Association meeting, addressed their President as "Mr President, Sir." Incidentally, the woman also speaks for divorce. Now let us look at the way Gokak describes her:

This girl is reformist, what we call as "*Gandu Rami*" [i.e., a
Kannada word equivalent to tomboy] ... Her dress has
reached the height of a joke. We already know that the English
dress is half-naked. But her dress was sky naked ... Her lips
had the red colour of a chilly. A *queer* person. Even the
clouded moon won't be as faded as her face! This *animal*
stood up and spoke belligerently.[20]

Here, the West gets associated with divorce and the Indian woman
dressed in Western clothes called *gandu rami*, a queer and an animal
with the above features. She becomes the symbol of colonialism, so
that the nationalists can carry their agenda of opposing the West by
constructing the other in a negative way to define itself positively. It
is not only that the woman is used as a site to carry out the Indian
man's opposition to colonialism, but the nationalist self that they
construct through their cultural transactions categorically excludes
women totally. The way the nationalists had resolved the question
of women was by redefining women; if women don't fit into their
definition of Indian women they would denounce it as Western
immediately. They wouldn't endorse the woman who is not amenable
for control by the new patriarchy that has emerged in the context
of modernity and nationalism.

Apart from this, Western women are generally represented as of
immoral character, being ever ready to seduce men at any time,
and to squeeze Indian men of their last penny. Indian men come to
England to study, but white women enslave them with their seductive
charm, making the Indian men forget their purpose and their country.
Gokak quotes a lot of instances to prove his theory of Western
women and Indian men.[21] While talking about an opera on Savitri
and describing the Western woman who had acted as Savitri, he
says: "She had wrapped herself in a blue sari like the present Hindu
girl but the pallu had come passing on the head. And her movement
and gestures were betraying Western woman's manliness."[22] Thus,

the Western woman becomes the epitome of manliness, representing the West as man, and Indian woman of streetva, of womanliness representing Indian culture.

Other than women's bodies there are other sites of cultural encounter as well where the making of the nationalist "self" and its "other" is sharply staged. Food is one such cultural marker that can easily be mobilized for constructs of "self" and "other." In the nineteenth and early twentieth centuries – for that matter, even to this day – as soon as the upper caste men enter the ship, the first thing they notice is the huge preparation of non-vegetarian food. They pick upon it to write in their diary or autobiography or in their letters to relatives, recounting how they struggled against it and finally obtained vegetarian food. Non-vegetarianism gets equated with Western materialism and violence, while vegetarianism gets constructed as the authentic Indian food, standing for non-violence, and consequently the site on which the Indian self must be constructed and staged. The debate between Bhaskara Raya and his mother in *Indira Bayi* over food is one such instance. This construction of the Indian self, thus, excludes the majority of people in India who eat meat, and the nature of the Indian nationalist self constructed by these upper caste men is such that it excludes the majority of the non-Brahmin castes from its discourse.

III

The travel writings and frames of analysis so far employed to discuss the construction of the nationalist identity in Kannada during the late nineteenth and early twentieth centuries are useful in understanding a pan-Indian nationalist discourse as characterized by Partha Chatterjee. However, being limited to them amounts to turning a blind eye to the differences and tensions that exist between Kannada nationalist discourse and the Indian nationalist discourse, and obviously cannot account for the way in which these tensions were resolved or still live in a kind of tension. It also overlooks the relationship between a language-based Kannada nationalist movement and a caste-based backward class movement in the context of Mysore province in the early decades of this century. The early part of the twentieth century saw the emergence of Kannada through the efforts of Christian missionaries. There was also the attempt, on the part of the colonial administration and native scholars towards making Kannada amenable to function in the roles that modernity expected of it. At the same time there was a parallel consciousness that was emerging in the form of bigger caste identities and class identities based on castes. For example, various castes of Veerashaiva, came together to form a bigger caste identity called Lingayat and formed an association to promote the interest of the members of that community in education and other related fields that were emerging in the context of modernity. Similarly Lingayats, Okkaligas (the two major land holding dominant castes of Karnataka), Kuruba and Muslim form an alliance to demand fair representation of their community members in administration and other state-owned enterprises. This alliance popularly known as backward class movement was successful in getting community representation in the administration in 1918 with the implementation of the recommendations of Miller's Committee by the King. Later this movement/alliance formed a political outfit to contest elections to the local bodies. This alliance had formed a political community that was striving for an egalitarian society within princely Mysore that certainly would have hindered/affected the formation of an imagined political community called India. This political outfit looked at the Indian National Congress as an organ of the Brahmin lobby till 1938. Till then the Indian National Congress had only a nominal presence in the princely Mysore region. We find little representation or discussion of the Backward Class movement in Kannada literary writings, which were almost entirely dominated by the upper castes.

Before 1956, Karnataka did not exist politically. Till it actually became an independent state, it was constructed as a cultural entity with a glorious past. It all started around the turn of the nineteenth century. The regions now under the State of Karnataka were earlier mainly under the control of various regimes. The Mysore province was under the Maharaja of Mysore; Mangalore, Coorg and Bellary were under the Madras Presidency; Bidar, Gulbarga and Raichur (Hyderabad-Karnataka region) were under the Nizam of Hyderabad; Belgaum, Dharwar and Karwar were under the Bombay Presidency. In addition, there were many independent small provinces between these regions. Unless we take into account the differences among these regions in our analysis of early twentieth century discourse such as Indian nationalist, Kannada nationalist and colonial discourses, we would not be able to reflect on the relationship between a pan-Indian nationalist identity and a Kannada nationalist identity vis-à-vis other identities that were based on caste, but struggled to eradicate the inequality that existed between them.

To account for these issues, it is not enough to look at travel writings of Europe by Indians. If we limit ourselves only to this body of work, we will be ignoring the complex matrix in which the Indian nationalist identity and the Kannada nationalist identity were embedded. For that, we have to look into other travel writings by Kannadigas, i.e., other than on Europe, because those travels also shaped the subjectivities of Kannada people during that period. Here I give an instance to show the necessity of evolving new theoretical and conceptual categories to study such a complex phenomenon. It would help place the early twentieth century discourses not in the binary matrix of the Empire and writing back to the Empire, but in a complex matrix that would help us to understand some of the present day problems in its historical nature.

Apart from travelling to Western countries, Kannadigas have also travelled to East Asian countries like Japan. Sir M Vishweswaraiah visited Japan thrice. We can say that the influence of Japan is felt more on the modernity project of Mysore as envisaged by Sir M Vishweswaraiah than that of England. During the colonial period, the Kannadigas of Mangalore and Mysore region went to Madras for higher studies, while the people from North Canara and North Karnataka province moved towards Bombay and Pune. The influence of the reformist movement, the Justice movement and the Dravidian movement can be seen in Mysore and Mangalore regions, while in the North Karnataka regions, it was more of a revivalist nationalist attitude due to their close proximity to Pune and Tilak. Thus, journeys to destinations across continents affected their subjectivities in different ways. An example of the emergence of Kannada nationalist identity can be seen in the account provided by Alura Venkat Rao.

Alura Venkat Rao, who is supposed to be one of the early voices in Kannada nationalist movement, belongs to North Karnataka. He studied in Bombay and Pune. In Pune, he was in association with Savarkar, who later spearheaded the Hindu revivalist, anti-Muslim movement.[23] He was also a close associate of Tilak, who linked Ganesh festivals with the anti-colonial nationalist movement. He writes in his autobiography about the formation of Kannada identity:

When we were in college (around 1900), we never thought of Karnataka as having a separate identity. It was just a part of Maharashtra in the political movement. Our students never had the concept of Karnataka in their mind. Not only just this, but there was not much interaction between Dharwad, Bijapur and Belgaum districts, and Karawara was almost a non-entity for us. Few individuals were working here and there, but they never knew each other sufficiently. The students, who had come to Pune, without being aware of it, slowly started developing a kind of "we" feeling with each other. Marathi people used to call us "Kannadi appaa." They had no intention of teasing us but they were discriminating against us. It served the cause of unity among Kannadigas.

Naturally Kannadigas started having their own mess clubs for food. But still we were not able to get rid of our infatuation for Marathi. The Brahmins were more close to Marathi people than to Lingayats.[24]

This clearly shows that the formation of a Kannada unity in North Karnataka has much to do with the discriminatory attitude practiced by the Marathi people in Pune. It cannot be simply described as anti-colonial in nature, and travelling to Pune is undoubtedly the cause of the formation of such an identity. The relation between Brahmins who identified themselves with the Marathi people rather than with the Kannada Lingayats adds a different perspective to the whole issue. Thus we need to come out of the binary of colonizer and the colonized to understand the construction of different subjectivities and take cognizance of the multiple "others" a single "self" might have had during the colonial period. For such an endeavour we need to look at not only the writings on travel to Europe but also within India and also within what was emerging as Karnataka.

Notes

1   For a fuller argument, see Talal Asad, "The Concept of Cultural Translation in British Social Anthropology," in James Clifford, ed, *Writing Culture: Politics and Poetics of Colonial Anthropology,* (New Delhi: Oxford University Press, 1989).

2   Edward Said, *Orientalism,* (London: Penguin, 1978). On the relationship between British literature and imperialism see Patrick Brantlinger, *Rule of Darkness: British Literature and Imperialism, 1830-1914,* (Ithaca, London: Cornell University Press, 1988).

3   Partha Chatterjee, *Nationalist Thought and the Colonial World: A Derivative Discourse?* (London: Zed Books, 1986), 30.

4   Partha Chatterjee, *Nationalist Thought and the Colonial World: A Derivative Discourse?* 38.

5   Partha Chatterjee, *Nationalist Thought and the Colonial World: A Derivative Discourse?* 40.

6   On colonialism and translation, see Cohn, Bernard S, "The Command of Language and the Language of Command," in Ranjit Guha, ed, *Subaltern Studies*

IV: Writings on South Asian History and Society, (New Delhi: Oxford University Press, 1985); Tejaswini Niranjana, *Siting Translation: History, Post-Structuralism and the Colonial Context*, (Berkeley: University of California Press, 1992).

7   I am grateful for this phrase to a lawyer, who, in a workshop on "Translating Translation: Theory, Practice and Context" organized by Anveshi, at Central Institute of English and Foreign Languages, Hyderabad, in January 1998, narrated his experience of translating a book on a famous criminal case in the West.

8   Kumkum Sangari, and Sudesh Vaid, eds, *Recasting Women: Essays in Colonial History*, (New Delhi: Kali for Women, 1989), 10.

9   Antoinette Burton, "Making a Spectacle of Empire: Indian Travellers in Fin-de-Siècle London," *History Workshop Journal*, 42, 126-146, 128, 1996. Here, it is apt to briefly touch upon the genre of autobiography in English written by Indians. Bolanath Chandra's *The Travels of a Hindoo to Various Parts of Bengal and Upper India* is supposed to be the early travel writing by an Indian in English. Chattrapati Rajaram, the Maharaja of Kolhapur's diary of his brief sojourn in Europe appeared under the title *Diary of the Late Rajah of Kolhapur* in 1832. R C Dutt's *Three Years in Europe*, Behramji Malabari's *The Indian Eye on English Life or Rambles of a Pilgrim Reformer*, P C Mazoomdar's *Sketches of a Tour Round the World*, Bhagvat Sinh Jee, the Thakur of Gondal's *Journal of a Visit to England in 1883*, Sambhu Chandra Mukherji's *Travels and Voyages between Calcutta and Independent Tipperah*, G Paramswarn Pillai's *London and Paris Through Indian Spectacles*, and T Ramakrishna Pillai's *My Visit to the West* are some of the texts that belong to this genre that came out in the nineteenth and early twentieth centuries. See M K Naik, *A History of Indian English Literature*, (New Delhi: Sahitya Academy, 1982).

10   Antoinette Burton, "Making a Spectacle of Empire: Indian Travellers in Fin-de-Siècle London," 126-146.

11   Gulvadi Venkat Rao, *Indira Bayi Athava Saddharma Vijaya*, (Manipala: Gulvadi Venkat Rao Smaraka Kendra, 1989).

12   Gulvadi Venkat Rao, *Indira Bayi Athava Saddharma Vijaya*, 106-113. All translations from Kannada, unless otherwise mentioned, are mine.

13   M G Rangaiah, "Shri Vishweswaraiahnavara Sallakshita Adhikara Nirvahana," in Masti Venkatesh Iyengar, ed, *Sir M Vishweswaraiah*, (Bangalore: Nava Jeevana Kaaryalaya Trust, 1990), 65-66.

14   D C Subbarayappa, "Shri Vishweswaraiahnavara Bali Kelasa Madiddara Savi Nenapu" (Kannada – "Sweet Memories of Working with Shri Vishweswaraiah"), in Masti Venkatesh Iyengar, ed, *Sir M Vishweswaraiah*, (Bangalore: Nava Jeevana Kaaryalaya Trust, 1990), 74.

15   D V Gundappa, "Diwan Rangacharlu," in H M Nayak, ed, *D V G Krithi Shreni*, Vol.4, (Kannada – *Complete Works of D V Gundappa*), (Bangalore: Department of Kannada and Culture, Government of Karnataka, 1994).

16   D V Gundappa, "Diwan Rangacharlu," 25-26.

17 V K Gokak, "Samudradaacheyinda," ("From the Other Side of the Ocean"), *Pravása Studies*, (Bangalore: IBH Prakashana, 1988), 11.

18 V K Gokak, "Samudradaacheyinda," 16-17

19 V K Gokak, "Samudradaacheyinda," 31, emphasis mine.

20 V K Gokak, "Samudradaacheyinda," 81, emphasis mine.

21 V K Gokak, "Samudradaacheyinda," 87-88, 108-109, 114, 168-173, 210.

22 V K Gokak, "Samudradaacheyinda," 156.

23 Alura Venkata Rao, *Nanna Jeevana Smrithigalu*, (Kannada – *Memoirs of My Life*), (Dhaarawada: Manohara Grantha Male, 1974), 54.

24 Alura Venkata Rao, *Nanna Jeevana Smrithigalu*, 67-68.

References

1 Asad, Talal, "The Concept of Cultural Translation in British Social Anthropology", in Clifford, 1989.

2 Bhabha, Homi K, *Location of Culture*, (London: Routledge, 1994).

3 Brantlinger, Patrick, *Rule of Darkness: British Literature and Imperialism, 1830-1914*, (Ithaca, London: Cornell University Press, 1988).

4 Burton, Antoinette, "Making a Spectacle of Empire: Indian Travellers in Fin-de-Siècle London." *History Workshop Journal* 42:126-146, 1986.

5 Chatterjee, Partha, *Nationalist Thought and the Colonial World: A Derivative Discourse?*, (London: Zed Books, 1986).

6 Chatterjee, Partha, "Nationalist Resolution of the Woman's Question," 1986, in Kumkum Sangari and Sudesh Vaid, eds.

7 Clifford, James, ed, *Writing Culture: Politics and Poetics of Colonial Anthropology*, (New Delhi: Oxford University Press, 1989).

8 Clifford, James and Vivek Dhareshwar, eds, *Travelling Theories, Travelling Theorists*, Volume Five of the *Inscriptions*, (Santa Cruz: Group for the Critical Study of Colonial Discourse and the Centre for Cultural Studies, UCSC, 1989).

9 Cohn, Bernard S, "The Command of Language and the Language of Command", 1985, in Ranjit Guha, *Subaltern Studies, IV.*

10 Dirlik, Arif, "The Postcolonial Aura: Third World Criticism in the Age of Global Capitalism," *Critical Inquiry* 20: 328-356, 1994.

11 Ghose, Indira, *The Power of the Female Gaze: Women Travellers in Colonial India*, (New Delhi: Oxford University Press, 1998).

12 Gokak, V K, *Samudradaacheyinda*, ("From the Other Side of the Ocean"), *Pravasa Studies*, (Bangalore: IBH Prakashana, 1988).

13 Guha, Ranjit, ed, *Subaltern Studies IV: Writings on South Asian History and Society*, (New Delhi: Oxford University Press, 1985).

14 Gundappa, D V, "Diwan Rangacharlu" 1994, in Nayak.

15   Iyengar, Masti Venkatesh, ed, *Sir M Vishweswaraiah*, (Bangalore: Nava Jeevana Kaaryalaya Trust, 1990).

16   Naik, M K, *A History of Indian English Literature*, (New Delhi: Sahitya Academy, 1982).

17   Nayak, H M, ed, *D V G Krithi Shreni*, Vol. 4, *Complete Works of D V Gundappa*, (Bangalore: Department of Kannada and Culture, Government of Karnataka, 1994).

18   Niranjana, Tejaswini, *Siting Translation: History, Post-Structuralism and the Colonial Context*, (Berkeley: University of California Press, 1992).

19   Pratt, Mary Louise, *Imperial Eyes: Travel Writing and Transculturation*, (London and New York: Routledge, 1992).

20   Rangaiah, M G, "Shri Vishweswaraiahnavara Sallakshita Adhikara Nirvahana", in Iyengar.

21   Rao, Gulvadi Venkat, *Indira Bayi Athava Saddharma Vijaya*, (Manipala: Gulvadi Venkat Rao Smaraka Kendra, 1989).

22   Said, Edward, *Orientalism*, (London: Penguin, 1978).

23   Sangari, Kumkum and Sudesh Vaid, eds, *Recasting Women: Essays in Colonial History*, (New Delhi: Kali for Women, 1989).

24   Subbarayappa, D C, "Shri Vishweswaraiahnavara Bali Kelasa Madiddara Savi Nenapu," in Iyengar.

25   Sunder Rajan, Rajeswari, "The Third World Academic in Other Places; or, the Postcolonial Intellectual Revisted", *Critical Inquiry* 23:596-616, 1997.

26   Tharakeshwar, V B, "Self-Translation: Politics of Colonial and Post-Colonial Cultural Transactions", paper presented at the Seminar on *English Literature and Indian Literature: Reception and Resistance* at the University of Delhi in November 1997.

27   Tharakeshwar, V B, "Translating Colonial Discourse: Power/Resistance in the Nationalist Context", paper presented at the Workshop on *Translating Translation: Theory, Practice and Context*, organized by Anveshi at CIEFL, Hyderabad, in January 1998.

28   Tharakeshwar, V B, "Translating Tragedy: Colonialism, Nationalism and B M Srikantia", Paper presented at the annual IACLALS Conference at M S University of Baroda on *Journeys and Destinations* in February 1998.

29   Venkata Rao, Alura, *Nanna Jeevana Smrithigalu*, (Dhaarawada: Manohara Grantha Male, 1974).

30   Vidyashankar, S, *Pravasodhyama Haagu Kannadadalli Pravasa Sahitya*, (Bangalore: Sneha Prakashana, 1991).

NARENDRA LUTHER

Muhammad Quli Qutb Shah (1580-1611) was the fifth and the most celebrated ruler of the Qutb Shahi dynasty of Golconda. On an auspicious day, according to Ferishta, "when the Moon was in the constellation of Leo, and Jupiter in its own mansion," the Sultan issued a decree that a new city be built outside the fort. It should be "unequalled in the world and a replica of paradise itself"[1] holds that the injunction to replicate paradise was taken literally by Mir Momin, the prime minister of the sultanate who was also director of the project. Accordingly, the plan of the city, which was ready in 1591, incorporated many of the features of the mythical Islamic heaven. A reading, amongst others, of Suras 47,14; 56; 28; 7,47; and 55 of the Quran gives a complete description of the Islamic heaven. In the plan of the city, according to the German scholar, Jan Pieper, the following features went to make the city "a replica of heaven":

Orientation of the city based on the *Kiblah* direction of the central mosque on the upper floor of Charminar.

A fountain in the centre of the four arches located about 76 meters north of Charminar. From this fountain named *Charsu-ka Houz* (fountain of four directions) radiated four channels in the four cardinal directions. This feature symbolized the fountain in the Quranic heaven from which flow four canals of pure water, pure milk, pure honey, and pure wine (Quran: 47,14). A defunct fountain called *Gulzar Houz* still exists at the same place.

Again, there are two mythical trees in heaven – *Sidr* and *Talh*. They don't exist on Earth. The impressive fountain had two types of trees – cocoanut, and betel nut palm to symbolize the two mythical trees (Quran, 56,28).

There are four arches at a distance of 76 meters north of Charminar. Two of these – the northern and southern – represented the wall which, according to the Quran (7, 47) encloses the abode of the blessed. They had royal guards corresponding to the fierce Quranic "Men of the Wall." The other two – eastern and western arches stood for the Quranic pleasures. The enormous gold curtains on the western arch flowing in the air and the *shehnai* players on the eastern arch filling the air with the "nasal" sounds of the instrument, are taken as the evocation of Sura 55 of the Quran.

Finally, in the Islamic heaven, there is not one garden, but many.[2]

As a matter of fact, the word for heaven in Arabic – *jannat* – also means garden. Paradise is also called the Garden of Eden. That explained the abundance of gardens and greenery in the new city. About three-square kilometres of habitation was surrounded by twenty three square kilometres of greenery and gardens.

As a prince, Muhammad Quli had fallen in love with a Hindu girl, Bhagmati. So when the city was ready, he dedicated it to his ladylove and called it Bhagnagar after her name. In 1596, the customary chronogram was drawn up. It was *Farkhunda Buniyad*. That yielded the year of the establishment of the city. The Persian title meant "the city of fortune," which is incidentally connoted by "Bhagnagar" also. The name seems to have changed to Hyderabad sometime in the seventeenth century, though, as will be noted from the accounts that follow, it continued to be used extensively till late nineteenth century.

The city was an emporium for diamonds mined in the Kulur mines in the interior. With the ports of Masulipatnam on the eastern coast, and Goa on the west under it, the capital city became an important centre for international trade. The Dutch, the Portuguese, the French and the British were all trying to establish their foothold on the southern coast of India controlled by the Sultan of Golconda. The Qutb Shahi dynasty acknowledged the overlordship of the Shah of Persia (modern Iran) which at that time was acknowledged as the font of knowledge and culture in the East. The Persians dominated the court and the administration of Golconda. There was thus not only a large presence of foreigners in the city, but also a constant traffic of visitors of all types – traders, missionaries, tourists, scholars and adventurers. Ferishta considered it bigger and better than Agra and Lahore – the great cities of the Mughals. While Indians visited the city routinely, a good number of foreigners visited it since its inception and some of them have left detailed, interesting and authentic accounts of their visits. This essay shall look in some detail at these accounts since they are comparative, and bring experiences of other world cities to bear upon their view of Hyderabad.

Seventeenth to Eighteenth Centuries

The spate of visitors to the city began in the seventeenth century.

They came from Iran, England, France, Holland, and Italy. They come from different backgrounds, had varied callings, and diverse interests.

The first to write about the city was Muhammad Qasim, popularly known as Ferishta. He was born at Astarabad, modern Iran. In 1589, aged seventeen, he proceeded to Bijapur and became a military captain under Ibrahim Adil Shah II.

His aim was to write a history of the conquests of Islam in India, and his patron gave him the necessary support for that purpose. He claims that he consulted thirty four books and other sources for completing his work.

He never visited Hyderabad. The city was less than twenty years old when he wrote about it:

> As the air of Golconda had become impure and unhealthy, Muhammad Quli built a magnificent city at a distance of eight miles, which he called Bhagnagar, after his favourite mistress; but this city has since received the name of Hyderabad, although one part of it still retains the former name of Bhagnagar. It is ten miles in circumference; and its principal streets, contrary to the other towns in India, are wide and clean; its air is healthy, and running streams are conveyed through some of the principal markets, on each side of which rows of trees are planted, affording a pleasing shade and sight, and the shops are all of solid masonry. The King's palace is described as the most beautiful and extensive in India.[3]

Next was an Englishman called William Methwold. He came to India in 1616 as a factor in the East India Company and was posted at Masulipatnam on the East Coast from 1618-1622. When he made his many visits to Hyderabad, he was in his mid-twenties, and the city was around thirty. See how he bears out its freshness:

153

A city for sweetnesse of ayre, conveniencie of Water, and fertility of soyle is accounted the best situated in India, not to speak of the King's Palace, which for bignesse and sumptuousnesse, in the judgment of such as have travelled India, exceedeth all belonging to the Mogull or any other Prince: it being twelve miles in circumference built all of stone, and within, the most eminent palaces garnished with massie gold in such things as we commonly use iron, as in barres of windows, bolts, and such like, and in all other points fitted to the majesty of so great a King, who in elephants and jewels is accounted one of the richest Princes of India.[4]

The Englishman was followed by a number of Frenchmen – Tavernier, Thevenot, and the Abbe Carre – and by an Italian, Manucci. Of these, the first two wrote at considerable length about Hyderabad.

Jean Baptiste Tavernier, born in 1605 in Paris, was a dealer in diamonds, although he posed as a gentleman-trader and not a merchant. He visited Golconda twice by different routes, once in 1648 and again in 1652. According to Dr V Ball who translated Tavernier's "Travels" into English, he was the "most renowned" traveller of the seevnteenth century.[5]

He had an acute sense of observation. He was also very systematic in his approach and kept a good record of the roads by which he travelled, the mode of transport, the cities through which he passed, and the formalities that he had to undergo:

Bhagnagar is the name of the capital town of this kingdom, but it is commonly called GOLCONDA from the name of the fortress, which is only 2 coss distant from it, and is the residence of the King ...

... The neighbouring country is a flat plain, and near the town you see numerous rocks as at FONTAINEBLEAU. A large

NARENDRA LUTHER,

river bathes a wall of the town on the southwest side, and
flows into the Gulf of Bengal close to MASULIPATNAM. You
cross it at BHAGNAGAR by a grand stone bridge, which is
scarcely less beautiful than the PONT NEUF at Paris. The
town is nearly the size of ORLEANS, well built and well
opened out, and there are many fine large streets in it ...

There are beautiful gardens, and such large trees, that it is a
matter for astonishment how these arches are able to carry
such a weight; and one may say in general terms that this
house has all the appearances of a royal mansion ...

In the first place, when a stranger presents himself at the
gates, they search him carefully to see if he has any salt or
tobacco, because these yield the principal revenue of the
King.

There are so many public women in the town, the suburbs
and in the fortress which is like another town, that it is
estimated that there are generally more than 20,000 entered
in the Darogha's register, without which it is not allowed to
any woman to ply this trade ...

In the cool of the evening you see them before the doors of
their houses, which are for the most part small huts, and
when the night comes they place at the doors a candle or a
lighted lamp for a signal. It is then, also, that the shops where
they sell tari are opened. King derives from the tax which he
places on this tari a very considerable revenue, and it is
principally on this account that they allow so many public
women, because they are the cause of the consumption of
much tari, those who sell it having for this reason their shops
in their neighbourhood.[6]

Jean Baptiste Thevenot, born in 1633, visited Golconda during

1665-66. He measured the distances between the landmarks of the city and described the difficulties he had to undergo during his travels and stay here. Says he:

> The capital city of this Kingdom is called *Bagnagar*, the *Persians* call it *Aider-abad*, it is ... situated Latitude of seventeen Degrees ten Minutes; in a very long plain, hemmed in with little Hills, some Cosses Distant from the Town which makes the Air of that Place very wholesome, besides that, the Countrey of *Golconda* lies very high. The Houses of the Suburbs, where we arrived, are only built of Earth and thatched with Straw, they are so low and ill contrived, that they can be reckoned no more than Huts. We went from one end to the other of that suburbs which is very long and stopt near the Bridge, which is at the farthest end of it. There we stayed for a note from *Cotuals* House to enter the Town, because of the Merchants Goods of the Caravan which were to be carried to the *Cotuals* House to be searched. But a *Persian* named *Ak-Nazar*, a favourite of the Kings, who knew the chief of the Caravan, became informed of its arrival, sent immediately a Man with orders, to let us enter with all the Goods, and so we past the Bridge, which is only three Arches over. It is about three Fathom broad and is paved with large flat Stones ... At the end of the Bridge, we found the Gates of the City, which are no more but Barriers: Being entered, we marched a quarter of an hour through a long Street with Houses on both sides, but as low as those of Suburbs, and built of the same materials, though they have very lovely Gardens.

> We went to a *Caravanseray* called *Nimet-ulla*, which has its entry from the same Street. Everyone took his lodging there, and I hired two little Chambers, at two *Roupies* a Month. The

town makes a kind of Cross, much longer than broad, and extends in a straight line, from the Bridge to the four Towers; but beyond these Towers the street is no longer streight. I measured the length of the Town ... found that BAGNAGAR was five thousand six hundred and fifty paces in length, to wit, two thousand four hundred and fifty from the bridge to the Towers.

That which is called the four Towers, is a square building, of which each face is ten Fathom broad, and about seven high ...

Besides the *Indian* Merchants that are at *Bagnagar*, there are many *Persians* and *Armenians*, ... There are many Franks also in the Kingdome but most of them are *Portuguese*, who have fled thither for Crimes they have committed. However, the English and Dutch have lately settled there; the last make great profits. They established a Factory there ... where they buy up for the Company, many *Chites* and other Cloaths, which they vent elsewhere in the *Indies*. They bring from *Masulipatan* upon Oxen the Goods which they know to be of readiest sale in *Bagnagar*, and other Towns of the Kingdom, as Cloves, Pepper, Cinnamon, Silver, Copper, Tin and Lead ...[7]

He endorsed Tavernier's observation about the abundance of public women and added his observation about the liberty enjoyed by women:

The common People give their Wives great Liberty: When a Man is to be Married, the Father and Mother of his Bride make him promise that he will not take it ill that his Wife go and walk through the Town, or visit her Neighbours, nay and drink Tary, a drink that the Indians of GOLCONDA are extremely fond of.[8]

The Abbe Carre, born about 1639, visited Golconda in 1673.

He talks of the two towns of Golconda and Bhagnagar. He recorded in his journal:

> It is a very spacious town, situated in a flat country, watered by a fine river. It is full of strangers and merchants that trade is carried on by foreigners and others without any or particular business. There is such a concourse of every kind of people, merchandise and riches, that the place seems to be the centre of all trade in the East.[9]

The Italian Niccolao Manucci ran away from Venice in 1653 at the age of fourteen. Starting as an artilleryman with the Mughal Emperor Shah Jahan's son, Dara Shikoh, and later Jai Singh, he became a physician and joined Shah Alam when the latter was appointed governor of the Deccan in 1678.[10] He later joined the last sultan of Golconda, Tana Shah, and was pursued by Shah Alam for desertion. His escape and pursuit by Shah Alam reads like a thriller. His account is noteworthy because of his description of how he was helped by fellow Christians and Europeans in his flight and how he masqueraded successfully as a physician. He described the story himself:

> Nor must I omit to mention how some Christians in the service of the Gulkandah King aware that I was seeking to escape from Shah Alam, came out to meet me and escort me, so as to take my side in case any of the Gulkandah troops attempted to interfere with me.
>
> ... Thus the king heard of my arrival. As his European physician, a Frenchman named Monsieur Destremon, was dead, the king sent for me to his presence. There, after some conversation, he directed me to go and bleed a woman in his harem, much cherished by him, because she knew where the treasures of the King of Gulkandah Cotobxa (Qutb Shah)

were concealed. She was a Georgian and so extremely stout, and the fat covered the veins so much, that blood could not be drawn from her except from the capillary veins ...[11]

He did such a good job of it that the Sultan, Abdullah Qutb Shah also wanted the same treatment for himself. However, he suspected that Manucci might be Shah Alam's agent and so might harm him. When the Sultan was pressurized to surrender Manucci to Shah Alam, a deal was worked out between the two.

> The information reached me when I was at cards, and suppressing my tribulation, I went on for some time with the game. I then went out and betook myself to the house of the Dutch envoy, who was then Lorenco Pit, and begged his assistance in this delicate situation. After that I sent for the Father Vicar of Gulkandah, named Frey Francisco, of the order of St Augustin and most earnestly entreated him to see Rustam Rao and procure leave to remove to Machhlipatnam a brother of his called Ausgustinho, who had fallen ill.[12]

The late Sir Jadunath Sarkar, the famous historian, has published two accounts by two French officers about Hyderabad in the middle of the seventeenth century.

According to the unpublished account of one officer in 1750,

> The city is large and beautiful ... This city is very unclean within; summer and winter alike it is always full of mud. When it rains the roads are covered ankle-deep with water. The inhabitants are Musalmans and Hindus: there are some white like the Europeans; they are very affable and most courteous ... There are in this city many other houses which are very old; that in which Mons. De Bussy (French General) resides is very much out of order ... next we pass over a bridge

which is very beautiful for these countries. It is tolerably long and wide, paved with free stone, and has some thirty arches. When one is outside the city, one may say that there are here nothing but groves ... and were it not for the walls the gate and the bridge – one might take the city for a tope ... There are many superb buildings with beautiful gardens outside the city; but they are extremely distant ... The gates (of the city) as of the fort are closed about 7 o' clock in the evening and are not opened till 9 o' clock in the morning or still later, and that too not without the order of the governor.[13]

Sarkar then quotes from the manuscript of Comte. L.-L. Dolisy De Modave. Except the main road leading to Char Kaman, he found the

... other roads of the city are small and very dirty. However, here are on all sides beautiful houses with gardens and fountains; but nearly all of them are deserted ... I have not seen the city where the manners and customs of the capital of the [Mughal] Empire are more carefully followed than in this one ...

If one were to judge its population from the incredible crowds which ceaselessly fill all the length of the main road, one would come to the conclusion that this city contains an enormous number of inhabitants. I have been assured that this number reaches 500,000 persons; but after examining the point carefully I am of the opinion there is only half [that number].

The city of Hyderabad is joined to a large suburb, which stands on the opposite side of the river, by a large stone bridge that passes in India for a very fine bridge. The name of the suburb is Aurangabad, but it is commonly designated the Karvan ...

The country around Hyderabad is a vast plain of which the surface is sown with hillocks, sufficiently high and all composed either of bed rock or of loose boulders of a monstrous thickness... However, this very plain presents enough of verdure, and here we find an air of freshness which one would not have naturally expected ...

We find here more Arabs and doctors [i.e., "ulama," theologians] than in any other city of India without excepting Delhi even.[14]

Sarkar then quotes the account from the itinerary of Lieutenant Colonel John Upton in April 1977.

The city, in general, is on the decline, except the *Chawk,* or *Grand Bazar*, which is full with very good shops and houses; there are sixteen other *bazars*, or markets, in the city; and it is said, that there were fifty two in the reign of Tana Shah.[15]

The reason for the "decline" referred to above was that after the Mughal conquest of Hyderabad in 1687, the city had ceased to be the capital. The capital of the Deccan province of the Mughals was Aurangabad. Because of that, most of the high officials and nobles had also shifted there leading to a comparative neglect of the city. However, the Nizam liked to stay at Hyderabad partly to be away from the Marathas, and partly to be "more in the centre of his dominions, and more convenient for sending troops to keep off his most restless and troublesome neighbour, Hyder Ali."[16]

It will be of interest to narrate here an incident, which occurred in 1798. It shows how the Residency was built, and also the Nizam's ignorance of the elementary principles of scale.

Since 1779, the British had stationed a Resident at Hyderabad. In the beginning, the role of the Resident was ambassadorial, but as British influence increased, the Resident became more powerful.

Captain James Kirkpatrick (Resident from 1798 to 1805), in keeping with the expanding and crucial role of the English agent, decided to build an official residence for himself. He sounded out the Prime Minister, who secured the Nizam's approval to the proposal in principle. When the plan was presented to the Nizam, he took one look at it and threw it away in horror. Crestfallen, Kirkpatrick asked the Prime Minister the reason for this summary rejection. He simply laughed. "Resident Bahadur," he chided, "you made the plan on the paper so big that it seemed equal to the size of His Highness's dominions. How could he agree to part with that?"[17]

Next time the Resident submitted the same proposal on a piece of paper the size of a visiting card. The Nizam readily agreed and Kirkpatrick then took up the project of building the Residency. The structure was so grand that while visiting the city in 1817, Sir John Malcolm called it a "palace" and in a letter to Lady Clive (wife of the Governor of Madras) remarked that "it is only surpassed in splendour and magnitude by the Government House in Calcutta. That in Madras cannot be compared to it."[18]

Nineteenth Century

During the middle Ages, highway robbery in India was rampant. One of the later forms it was to assume, was what has been called Thugee. According to Meadows Taylor, "the word Thug means a deceiver, from the Hindee word Thunga, to deceive."[19] He attributed it to the division of India into numerous kingdoms and principalities, and the absence of roads, and in consequence, of public conveyance. Thugs were thieves who took travelling groups into confidence, then murdered them by throttling them with their handkerchiefs, buried their bodies and looted their belongings. In many cases, the local chiefs colluded with them. Its practitioners were both Hindus and Muslims. Interestingly, both worshipped goddess Bhavani and sought her blessings both before and after the heinous act.

Till 1811 the British authorities in India did not know about the prevalence of Thugee. In that year, following the disappearance of many army men during their official journeys, the commander-in-chief issued an order warning the soldiers against thugs. In 1812, the first assault on thugs was made following upon the murder of Lieutenant Monsell. Many thugs were killed.[20]

Lord William Bentinck, Governor General of India (1828-35) launched a vigorous, systematic and long drawn-out campaign against Thugee in 1830. Colonel Sleeman was put in charge of the operations. During 1831 to 1837, Taylor says, on the testimony of Captain Reynolds, that a total number of 412 thugs were hanged, 1059 transported to Penang et cetera, 87 given life sentence, 483 made approvers, and many given various terms of imprisonment. He puts the total number of cases dealt with at 3266.[21]

Taylor wrote his novel *Confessions of a Thug* based upon the story of one of the convicted thugs, Ameer Ali. In the introduction to the book, Taylor claims that the story described by him

Is, alas; almost all true. What there is of fiction has been supplied only to connect the events, and make the adventures of Ameer Ali as interesting as the nature of his horrible profession would permit me.[22]

However, we will do well to remember that Taylor himself was an Assistant Resident at Hyderabad. It is very likely, therefore, that the descriptions of some of the sites and incidents of Hyderabad in the book are based upon his observations.

Ameer Ali's description of the Husain Sagar Lake seems entirely credible, particularly if he had not seen any sea:

We stood for a long time gazing upon the beautiful prospect, so new to us all, and wondering whether the sea, of which we had heard so much, could be anything like what was before us. When I saw it first, me thought I could have fallen down and worshipped it. It appeared so illimitable, its edge touching as it were the heavens, and spread out into an expanse, which the utmost stretch of my imagination could not compass.[23]

He was swept off his feet when he had the first glimpse of the city from the vantage point of Naubat Pahad, which is now occupied by the Venkateswara Temple:

Hyderabad ... the first city of the Dukhun, justly celebrated throughout the countries I had passed ... its white terraced houses gleaming brightly in the sunlight from amidst what seemed to me at the distance almost a forest of trees. The Char Minar and Mecca Masjid rose proudly from the masses of buildings by which they were surrounded; and here and there a white dome, with its bright gilt spire, marked the tomb of some favourite or holy saint, while smaller mosques, I might say in hundreds, were known by their slender white minarets ...

The city seemed to be of immense extent; but I thought from the number of trees that it was composed principally of gardens and enclosures, and was much surprised afterwards, when I entered it, to find its streets so filled with houses, and the whole so thickly peopled.

It was altogether a most lovely scene: the freshness of the morning, the pureness of the air, and the glittering effects of the city and its buildings caused an impression that can never be effected from my memory ...

To see this alone is worth a journey from Delhi.[24]

He was one of the few to have visited the Qutb Shahi tombs. They were "dark and gloomy and filled with bats and wild pigeons whose cooing re-echoed within the lofty domes – and others whose wide arches admitted the light of the day, and were more cheerful in appearance."[25]

The following interesting accounts by a military officer, Captain R F Burton, and his wife were carried by the *Times of India* in its issues of 11th March and 29th March 1876.

First, the issue of 11th March –

A Ride through Hyderabad

We have just returned from our first survey of the "Lion City."[26]

The country about Hyderabad in the Dekhan is very picturesque. Nowhere more decided contrasts of sun-burnt granite and syenite in bristling ridges, solitary boulders, loggan-stones, weathered into likeness of man and beast, castellated rocks piled as by the hands of art; in ruddy fallows, in little green paddy fields, in sky blue distances, in golden stubbles almost pulverised by burning sun and deficient showers, in glorious "topes" of mangoes, tamarinds and shady wild figs ...

Here we have our first view of the city, whose crumbling towers and ramparts, abutting upon the right bank of the River Valley, contrast queerly with the prim Gothic battlements of the North-Eastern or Palace Gate; its neighbour is the Delhi or Water Gate, where elephants are taken down to bathe ...

There is no pavement except in patches of black basalt, which reminded my wife of the Salahiyyah Causeway at Damascus, and in places the original granite still outcrops in uninjured boulders.

Clerical and civilian garb; of dark Portuguese and sallow Eurasians; of Parsees whose hats look like chimney pots

165

blown backwards by a gale of wind; of Banyas with beaked turbans red and gold; of Marathas, whose head gear assumes the dimensions of tea tables; and of Moslems clad in costumes almost as numerous as the individuals that wear them. Here the chief foreign items are dark, wiry Arabs from Hazramaut or the Persian Gulf; sturdy Sulaymanis or Afghans, and large limbed Zanzibarian Sidis (Wasawahili), sometimes pur sang, oftener mixed with Asiatic blood; the Wahabis conceal their tenets ...[27]

On 29 March 1876:

... The vulgar of Hyderabad, unlike most Moslem cities in India, are less fond of kite flying and of pigeon-tumbling than of cock-fighting, while the latter is ignored by the higher classes ... Here there are five or six cockpits, especially that of kachi-Ghora (Kachiguda), where mains are fought every Sunday. The bird is large, often weighing 5 to 5½ seers (10 to 11 lbs.), equalling, in fact, a small turkey; it is one of the best in India; the price reaches Rs 200. You cannot depend upon your friend to send or to sell you an Asil or thoroughbred ... the birds are trained, physicked and sweated with more care than Spaniards or Mexicans can bestow upon them, and they are heated with Masala (spices), whose preparation is a secret, that they will fly at man or beast ... The experienced "Murghbaz" (cock-fighter) will have dozens of these articles, showing every variety length, weight and angle.[28]

The thug and the army officer also took note, inter alia, of a very picturesque geophysical feature of Hyderabad – its two and a half billion year old gneissic rocks.

Before closing the century, it may be worth looking at the observation of two more visitors. That is because they give us a different perspective – on the social life of the city.

In 1876, Val C Prinsep, the British painter, was commissioned to paint a picture for the Government of India, as a present for Queen Victoria on the assumption of the title of Empress of India. The subject was the Imperial Assemblage of Delhi. He took the opportunity to visit a number of important cities of India, including Hyderabad. The Nizam of Hyderabad at that time was Mir Mehboob Ali Khan, a boy of about eleven. During his visit, he kept a journal, which was published as a book: *Imperial India – An Artist's Journals.* He noticed that

> Etiquette is very strict here. The amount of bowing and *salaaming* at the Minister's (Sir Salar Jung I) is most embarrassing. A younger brother is not allowed to sit in the presence of his elder, and *salaams* to the ground on coming to the room. I have been told that when a boy is born, eight wet nurses are chosen for him, and generally succeed in killing him with over-nourishment, as might be expected. The late Nizam died in a singular and most depressing way. He had a disease, not dangerous of itself, but one which rendered a slight operation necessary: but he funked. He had all the people of the city who were afflicted with the same disease brought to him and operated on in his presence; yet he could not make up his mind, and at last mortification set in, and he died miserably.

This story of the etiquette of the Nizam's Court will, I hope, prove interesting. When the Nizam was paying a visit to Golconda, he, boy-like, ran into Sir Salar Jung's room and found the Minister taking *siesta.* The Minister had taken off his girdle! Now to be in the Nizam's company without a girdle is a heinous offence, and the Minister at once handed over to the little Nizam fifteen gold *mohurs.* The next morning he sent him 1,500 rupees to complete the fine! What do you think they call this girdle, which is generally a golden kind of sword-belt? *Buggelas* (Actually Bugloos), which they say is an English word. Can it be derived from "buckles"?

The Hyderabadists (Sic) are, like the natives, mad on the subject of glass chandeliers. They have them even in the mosques, and when they are tied in muslin bags they have anything but a religious look, but rather as the family were out of town.[29]

Apart from the host of commoners, some members of the European royalty also visited Hyderabad. Prince Albert Victor came in 1893, while the future King George V came with his wife in 1905 when he was Prince of Wales. In 1893, came the Archduke Franz Ferdinand, heir apparent to the throne of Austria. He kept a diary of his journey. In that he gives authentic information about Hyderabad and Nizam VI. He was taken for shikar outside the city. On return, it was proposed that he and the Nizam have a shooting match. They were to shoot clay balls placed on the neck of several bottles placed at a distance of thirty steps, and bottles and coins flung into the air.

We had to shoot the clay balls without hitting the bottles. The Nizam shot first and missed four clay balls; I followed, and hit three out of four, whereupon the Nizam and his retinue burst into an applause ... Then came the most difficult part, that is the shooting of rupees thrown into the air. Each marksman had eight shots. The Nizam hit one, and I was lucky to hit three, though I had no experience of that earlier. The Nizam was very sporting and showed his appreciation although it was the first time that he had been beaten at the game. I must admit that deep inside I felt as proud as lion.[30]

The Archduke also visited the famous palace of Asman Jah, the Prime Minister (1884-94). In the courtyard there were five chained tiger cubs. Asman Jah had shot the mother the previous year and brought the cubs home. They played like kittens. "They were tame so that one could fondle them. To my delight the Prime Minister presented two of them to me, which I hope will reach Vienna safely." [31]

The translator of the diary, Mrs Elizabeth Al-Himrani checked the records of the Vienna Zoo and found that two cubs had indeed been donated to it in 1893.

Twentieth Century

There are other accounts in the twentieth century during the first half of which Hyderabad was called "a bride amongst the cities" by Urdu writers and poets from the north. It had been rebuilt after the Great Floods of 1908 on the basis of the plans prepared by Visveswarayya.

J P L Gwynn, an ICS officer who served in the old Madras (now Tamil Nadu) state, and later in Andhra Pradesh, visited Hyderabad in 1943. He recalled "the quiet and peaceful atmosphere of the old city of Hyderabad, so different from the hustle and bustle of today. I have a distinct impression that gentlemen walking about in their everyday costume wore sword belts with swords dangling from them." [32] He contrasted the difference in the architecture of Hyderabad and Secunderabad.

> I will not discuss Secunderabad's architecture in detail. It became the largest military cantonment in India with its building conforming to the all-India type designs drawn up in the periods when those buildings were erected. Collectively, they (the cantonment architecture of Secunderabad) represent quite well the character of those times (when they were constructed), but individually – take Secunderabad Club, for example – they are utilitarian and featureless. A point to be

mentioned here is the notable contrast in appearance between the streets of Secunderabad and Hyderabad ... Basically the reason for the contrast is that residences built in Secunderabad were of the bungalow type, while in Hyderabad they were of the urban house type. The very visible sign of the contrast is that Secunderabad houses have front verandas while those of Hyderabad do not.³³

Philip Mason of the ICS, retiring prematurely and on his way to England in 1947, stopped for a while in Hyderabad at the request of Princess Durreshahwar. His autobiographical *A Shaft of Sunlight* (1978) shows how impressed – and confused – he was by the cosmopolitan character of the city. His surprise is indeed surprising since he had served in the present state of Uttar Pradesh for a long time. He attended a birthday party in Hyderabad:

"Who is that little boy?" I asked my nearest neighbour and she told me a name I have forgotten, but a name unmistakably Hindu, some Ram Swarup, or Jag Deo.

"But he is wearing the wrong sort of hat!" I exclaimed in astonishment. He was wearing a Turkish fez, like an involuted red pot with a black silk tassel, which in Northern India was always the sign of a Muslim. "Oh, in Hyderabad we do not care for things like that!" said my neighbour gaily. "It is one of the nice things here that we are so delightfully cosmopolitan."³⁴

Alan Champbell Johnson, in his *Mission with Mountbatten* (1952) gives a fleeting glimpse of his flying visit to Hyderabad in 1947. He describes his meeting with Nizam VII, his personality, and his drawing room. Harriet Ronken Lynton (with Mohini Rajan) wrote about the Hyderabad of the Sixth Nizam (d. 1911). Their book, *The Days of the Beloved* published in 1974, gives a chatty account of a fascinating period in which the ruler went round the city incognito at night, and made generous gifts impulsively. Professor Karen Leonard formerly of the University of California, Los Angeles has a fascination for Hyderabad and has made many trips to the city. Her *Social History of an Indian Caste: The Kayasths* (1978) and her numerous articles published in leading journals give a fascinating account of many aspects of Hyderabad, including the "composite" character of the administration of Hyderabad under the Asaf Jahs. The Australian author, Ian Austin, has recounted many stories and legends in his book, *The City of Legends*, based on oral testimony.

The most recent to join the procession is William Dalrymple. He has written about Hyderabad with much the same enchantment as is found in the narration of earlier chroniclers. Though his focus is the romance of James Achilles Kirkpatrick, the British Resident in Hyderabad from 1798 to 1805, and Khairunissa, he gives interesting details about the city from the time that it was founded, citing many of his remote predecessors approvingly. His book, *White Mughals* is marked by references to primary sources and adds to the corpus of important literature about the city.

It is noteworthy that all these chroniclers testified to the original name of the city, Bhagnagar – its detailed town planning, its architecture, its grandeur, its greenery, good climate, large size and the cosmopolitan character of the population. Visitor after visitor has referred to the gardens not only in the city, but also in individual houses in the city. Rafi-ud-Din Shirazi in his *Tazkirat-ul Muluk* said in 1608 that "both bazaars and houses are so full of trees that the whole city looks like one garden."[35] Ameer Ali more than two hundred years later also spoke likewise. Tavernier, Thevenot and Abbe Carre spelt the name of the city as "Bagnagar." That led one modern historian, late Professor Haroon Khan Sherwani to claim, in another context, that Tavernier did so because the city was full of gardens (Bagh in Urdu).[31] Ferishta and Methwold declared that in its grandeur it was

171

better even than the great Mughal cities. Tavernier found it the size of Orleans in France, "well built and well opened out."³⁶ The French travellers praised the *Purana Pull* – the bridge constructed by Ibrahim Quli Qutb Shah in 1578, and the only one in existence till the nineteenth century – and it was compared by Tavernier to the new bridge in Paris. An anonymous French officer visiting it in 1750 found it "very beautiful for these countries."³⁷ Of course, while the main thoroughfare was good, some chroniclers have drawn our attention to the dirty and unpaved streets. Nawab Sarvar-ul-Mulk, in his autobiography confirmed in that the street leading to the royal stables was so filthy that, it was known as "Muthri Galli" (the Urinating lane). The efforts of Salar Jung in the second part of the nineteenth century to improve the sanitation were thwarted by his rivals by leading Nizam V to believe that Salar Jung was trying to do that to facilitate the entry of the British into the city.³⁸

Another thread that runs through the chronicle is that Golconda/ Bhagnagar/Hyderabad was an important commercial centre. In 1673 Abbe Carre found there "such a concourse of every kind of people, merchandize and riches, that the place seems to be the centre of all trade in the East."³⁵ In a commercial centre, the coexistence of people of different nationalities is inevitable. We find that certified by practically all the visitors. Abbe Carre recorded in his diary on 14ᵗʰ March 1673, that due to his recent illness at Bijapur, he stayed with a Portuguese priest – who was a vicar of the Golconda Mission and whose house and church were in the suburb called Millipore.³⁹ We have seen above the reference made by Niccolao Manucci to the many Christians who were in the service of the Sultan of Golconda. Readers will note that he got the job of a French physician of the Sultan who had died. He was able to escape from Golconda due to the influence of the Dutch envoy and the Father Vicar of Golconda. All these elements go into the making of a cosmopolitan city.

One of the characteristics of a cosmopolitan city is the presence of women of pleasure. Tavernier estimated their number at 20,000 and Thevenot seemed to concur without quoting a definite number. From the sources available, one might infer that prostitution had been in existence for some time, and had its own well-entrenched mechanisms. Also, the large consumption of Tary (Toddy, or country liquor), added significantly to the revenues of the state, a nexus which is very familiar even today.

However, no other foreign chronicler supports Thevenot's observation that women enjoyed great liberty. There is little historical or sociological evidence to warrant this conclusion, and it is possible that his view of the situation was based solely on the behaviour of the public women he encountered.

In some comments made by foreign observers, we find interesting social comments. The acquisition of Residency land by the Nizam, the strict court etiquette, and the extravagant lifestyle of the Nizams also emerge from some of the later chronicles of visitors. That provides a totally different view of the city.

Hyderabad continues to be visited by foreigners. Some of them take notes and even write articles about it in papers back home. Lately, television documentaries by foreign channels seem to have overtaken accounts in black and white. We can only hope that the authors of travelogues and memoirs will not cease to record their impressions for future generations in the old trusted and long lasting medium of print.

Notes

1   Mohd Kasim Ferishta, *History of the Rise of the Mohammedan Power in India (Till 1612)*, Vol. III, Translated by John Briggs, (London: Longman, Rees, Orme, Brown & Green, 1829), 1908, Volume II, 173.

2   Jan Pieper, *Hyderabad: A Quranic Paradise in Architectural Metaphors* in A Peruccioli, ed, (Genzano de Roma: Environmental Design, The Journal of the Islamic Environmental Design Research Centre, January 1983), 46-51.

3. *Ferishta*, Translated by John Briggs, 1829, Vol III, 335.

4   As quoted in W M Moreland, Relations of Golconda in the Early Seventeenth Century (AD 1608-1622), (London: Hakluyt Society, 931), 23.

5   V Ball, *Travels in India* by Jean-Baptiste Tavernier, William Brooke, Reprint ed, (Atlantic: 1889), 1.

6   Ball, *Travels in India,* 152-158.

7   Mons de Thevenot, *The Travels into the Levant.* Vol. *III,* Translated by A Lovell, (London: H Paul, 1687), 94-97.

8   Thevenot, *The Travels into the Levant,* 94.

9   Abbe, Carre, *The Travels of Abbe Carre in India in the New East 1672-74,*Vols I & II, 1674, (Delhi: Asian Educational Services), 329.

10   Niccolao Manucci, *Storia Do Mogor,* 1705, Translated by William Irvine, (London: John Murray, 1913), v-vi.

11   Niccolao Manucci, *Storia Do Mogor,* 192.

12   Niccolao Manucci, *Storia Do Mogor,*195.

13   Sir Jadunath Sarkar, "Haidarabad and Golconda in 1750 as seen through French Eyes," Islamic Culture, Vol. X, April 1936, 234-47.

14   Sir Jadunath Sarkar, "Haidarabad and Golconda in 1750 as seen through French Eyes," 523-26.

15   Sir Jadunath Sarkar, "Old Hyderabad," *Islamic Culture,* Vol X, 1937, 527.

16   Sir Jadunath Sarkar, "Old Hyderabad,"526-27

17   John William Kaye, *Life and Correspondence of Major – General John Malcolm,* (Smith Elder & Co; 1856), 100-101.

18   H G Briggs, *The Nizam – His History and Relations with the British Government,* (Bernard Quatrich, 1861), 100.

19   Philip Meadows Taylor, *Confessions of a Thug,* (London: 1839), Reprint, (New Delhi: Asia Educational Services, 1988), 3.

20   Philip Meadows Taylor, *Confessions of a Thug,* 12.

21   Philip Meadows Taylor, *Confessions of a Thug,* 17-18.

22   Philip Meadows Taylor, *Confessions of a Thug,* 102.

23   Philip Meadows Taylor, *Confessions of a Thug,* 102.

24   Philip Meadows Taylor, *Confessions of a Thug,* 102-105.

25   Philip Meadows Taylor, *Confessions of a Thug,* 149.

26   Literal translation of Hyderabad – Hyder being Ali who is referred to as the Lion of Islam.

27   *Hyderabad Affairs* III, 335-339.

28   *Hyderabad Affairs* III, 345.

29   Val C Prinsep, *Imperial India – An Artist's Journals,* (Chapman And Hall, undated.), 316-317.

30   Archduke Franz Ferdinand, *My Journey Around the World,* (Vienna: Franz Ferdinand Museum 1895), Translated by Elizabeth Al-Himrani, (Vienna: 1996), 20.

31   Archduke Franz Ferdinand, *My Journey Around the World,* 20.

32 J P L Gwynn, "Conservation of Historical Monuments in Hyderabad," in *Hyderabad – 400 – Saga of a City*, ed, K S S Seshan, (Hyderabad: Association of British Council Scholars, 1993), 4-5.

33 J P L Gwynn, "Conservation of Historical Monuments in Hyderabad," 4-5.

34 Philip Mason, *A Shaft of Light: Memoirs of a Varied Life*, (Vikas, 1978) Page no. not available.

35 Rafi-ud-Din Shirazi, *Tazkirat-ul-Muluk*, Ms. Fol. 61 b. State Central Library, '1608, as quoted in H K Sherwani, *Muhammad-Quli Qutb Shah – Founder of Hyderabad*, (City: Asia Publishing House, 1967)

36 Jean Baptiste Tavernier, *The Six Voyages*, Vol. I *(1676)*, Translated by V Ball, (London: Macmillan & Co., 1889), 123.

37 Sir Jadunath Sarkar, "Haidarabad and Golconda in 1750 as Seen Through French Eyes," 241.

38 Nawab Bahadur Sarvar-ul-Mulk, *My Life*, Translated by Nawab Jiwan Yar Jung Bahadur, (London: Arthur H Stockwell, 1932), 91-92.

39 Abbe Carre, *The Travels of Abbe Carre in India in the New East 1672-74*, Vol. II, 329.

References

1 Abbe Carre. *The Travels of the Abbe Carre in India and the Near East, 1672-74*, Vols. I & II, Compiled by Lady Fawcett, London, Reprint, (New Delhi: Asia Educational Services, 1990).

2 Archduke Franz Ferdinand, *My Journey Around the World*, (Vienna: Franz Ferdinand Museum, 1895), Translated by Elizabeth Al-Himrani, (Vienna: 1996).

3 Austin, Ian, *The City of Legends*, (Delhi: Viking, 1992).

4 Bernier, Francis, *Travels in the Mughal Empire*, Vols I & II, Translated by Irving Brock, (London: William Pickering,1826).

5 Briggs, H G, *The Nizam – His History and Relations with the British Government*, Vols I & II, (London: Bernard Quatrich, 1861), Reprint, (New Delhi: Rupa & Co., 2002).

6 Carre, Abbe, 1674, *The Travels of Abbe Carre in India in the New East 1672-74*, Vols I & II, Reprint, (Delhi: Asian Educational Services, 1990).

7 Dalrymple, William, *White Mughals*, (London: Viking, 2002).

8 Ferishta, Mohd Kasim, *History of the Rise of the Mohammedan Power in India (Till 1612)*, Vol. III, Translated by John Briggs, (London: Longman, Rees, Orme, Brown & Green. 1829).

9 Gwynn, J P L, "Conservation of Historical Monuments in Hyderabad" in *Hyderabad – 400 – Saga of a City*, (Hyderabad: Association of British Council Scholars, ed, K S S Seshan, 1993).

10 *Hyderabad Affairs*, Vol. III, 1876, (Andhra Pradesh State Archives, Hyderabad).

11 Johnson, Alan Champbell, *Mission with Mountbatten*, (London: Robert Hale, 1952).

12 Kaye, John William, *Life and Correspondence of Major – General John Malcolm*, (London: Smith Elder & Co., 1856).

13 Leonard, Karen Isaken, *Social History of an Indian Caste: The Kayasths*, (University of California Press, 1978), Reprint, (Hyderabad: Orient Longman, 1994).

14 Luther, Narendra, *Prince Poet Lover Builder – Muhammad Quli Qutb Shah – The Founder of Hyderabad*, (New Delhi: Publications Division, Government of India, 1991).

15 Luther, Narendra, *Hyderabad: Memoirs of a City*, (Hyderabad: Orient Longman, 1995).

16 Lynton, Harriet Ronken and Mohini Rajan, *The Days of the Beloved*, (University of California Press, 1974).

17 Manucci, Niccolao, *Storia Do Mogor*, Translated by William Irvine, (London: John Murray, 1913).

18 Mason, Philip, *A Shaft of Light: Memoirs of a Varied Life*, (Mumbai: Vikas, 1978).

19 Moreland, W M, *Relations of Golconda in the Early Seventeenth Century (AD 1608-1622)*, (London: Hakluyt Society, 1931).

20 Pieper, Jan, *Hyderabad: A Quranic Paradise in Architectural Metaphors*, (Genzano de Roma: Environmental Design, The Journal of the Islamic Environmental Design Research Centre, January 1983).

21 Prinsep, Val C, *Imperial India – An Artist's Journals*, (London: Chapman And Hall, Undated).

22 Sarkar, Sir Jadunath, "Haiderabad and Golconda in 1750 as Seen Through French Eyes," (Hyderabad: Islamic Culture, Vol. X, April 1936).

23 Sarkar, Sir Jadunath, *Old Hyderabad*, (Hyderabad: Islamic Culture, Vol. XI, October 1937).

24 Sarvar-ul-Mulk, Nawab Bahadur, *My life*, Translated by Nawab Jiwan Yar Jung Bahadur, (London: Arthur H Stockwell, 1932).

25 Sherwani, H K, *Muhammad Quli Qutb Shah – Founder of Hyderabad*, (Bombay: Asia Publishing House, 1967).

26· Shirazi, Rafi-ud-Din, *Tazkirat-ul- Muluk*, 1608, Ms. Fol. 61 b. State Central Library, (Quoted by Sherwani).

27 Tavernier, Jean Baptiste, *The Six Voyages, Vol. 1 (1676)*, Translated by V Ball, (London: Macmillan & Co., 1889).

28 Taylor, Philip Meadows, *Confessions of a Thug*, (London: 1839), Reprint, (New Delhi: Asia Educational Services, 1988).

29 Thevenot, Mons de, *The Travels into the Levant, Vol. III*, Translated by A Lovell, (London: H Paul, 1687).

SELECT BIBLIOGRAPHY

1   Ackerley, J R, *Hindoo Holiday: An Indian Journal,* *(London*: Penguin, 1932).

2   Adams, Percy G, *Travel Literature and the Evolution of the Novel*, (Kentucky: The University of Kentucky Press, 1983).

3   Appleton, Jay, *The Experience of Landscape*, (Chichester: John Wiley and Sons Limited, 1996).

4   Ceasar, Terry, *Forgiving the Boundaries: Home as Abroad in American Travel Writing,* (London: University of Georgia Press, 1995).

5   Craig, Patricia, *The Oxford Book of Travel Stories*, (Delhi: Oxford University Press, 1996).

6   Dalrymple, William, *At the Court of Fish-Eyed Goddess: Travels through the Indian Subcontinent*, (New Delhi: Harper Collins, 1999).

7   Driver, Felix, *Geography Militant: Cultures of Exploration and Empire*, (Massachusetts: Blackwell Publishers, 2001).

8   Dyson, Ketaki Kushari, *A Various Universe: A Study of the Journals*

and Memoirs of British Men and Women in the Indian Subcontinent, 1765-1856, (New Delhi: Oxford University Press, 1980).

9   Edney, Matthew H, *Mapping an Empire: The Geographical Construction of British India*, (London: Oxford University Press, 1997).

10   Fraser, Keith, *Worst Journeys: A Picador Book of Travel*, (Delhi: Rupa and Co., 1993).

11   Fussell, Paul, *Abroad: British Literary Travelling Between the Wars*, (New York: Oxford University Press, 1980).

12   Ghose, Indira, ed, *Memsahibs Abroad: Writings by Women Travellers in Nineteenth Century India,* (Delhi: Oxford University Press, 1998).

13   Greenblatt, Stephen, *Marvellous Possessions: The Wonder of the New World*, (Oxford Clarendon Press, 1991).

14   Greenfield, Bruce, *Narrating Discovery: The Romantic Explorer in American Literature, 1790-1855*, (New York: Columbia University Press, 1992).

15   Hassam, Andrew, "Narrative Occasions and the Quest for Self-Presence in the Travel Diary," *Ariel: A Review of International English Literature*, The University of Calgary Press, Vol 2, No 4, October, 1990.

16   Higgonet, Margaret, Joan R Templeton, eds, *Reconfigured Spheres: Feminist Explorations of Literary Space*, (Amherst: University of Massachusetts Press, 1994).

17   Housden, Roger, *Travels through Sacred India,* (London: Thorsons, 1996).

18   Huxley, Aldous, *Beyond the Mexique Bay*, (New York: Harper & Brothers, 1934).

19   Innes, A Sherrie, Diana Royer, eds, *Breaking Boundaries: New Perspectives of Women's Regional Writing,* (Iowa City: University of Iowa Press, 1997).

20   Jackson, John Brickerhoff, *Discovering the Vernacular Landscape*,

(New Haven and London: Yale University Press, 1984).

21   Kampuchen, Amrtin, *My Broken Love: Günter Grass in India and Bangladesh*, (Delhi: Penguin Books).

22   Kaey, Julia, *With Passport and Parasol: Adventures of Seven Victorian Ladies,* (London: Penguin Books and BBC Books, 1994).

23   Khilnani, Sunil, *The Idea of India*, (London: Penguin Books, 1998).

24   Kolodny, Annette, *The Lay of the Land: Metaphor as Experience and History in American Life and Letters*, (Chapel Hill: The University of North Carolina Press, 1975).

25   Kroller, Eva-Marie, "Rhetorical Strategies in Travel Writing by Victorian Women," *Ariel: A Review of International English Literature*, The University of Calgary.

26   Lewis, Norman, *A Goddess in the Stones*, (New Delhi: Rupa, 1991).

27   Margaret, Macmillan. *Women of the Raj*, (London: Thames and Hudson, 1996).

28   Menon, Dilip, "Traveller as Historian," *The Hindu Literary Supplement*, 2nd September, 2001.

29   Midgley, Clare, *Gender and Imperialism*, (Manchester and New York: Manchester University Press, 1998).

30   Muir, Richard, *Approaches to Landscape*, (London: Macmillan Press Ltd, 1999).

31   Murray, Jack, *The Landscapes of Alienation: Ideological Subversion in Kafka*, (Stanford: Stanford University Press, 1991).

32   Naipaul, V S, *An Area of Darkness*, (London: Penguin, 1964).

33   Naipaul, V S, *India: A Wounded Civilization*, (Harmondsworth: Penguin 1977).

34   Newby, Eric, *Slowly Down the Ganges*, (London: Picador, 1968).

35   Onkar, Deepa, *The Writing of History in the Travel Narratives of Michael Wood: Blurring the Boundaries?* Unpublished M.Phil Dissertation, University of Hyderabad.

36   Osborne, Peter D, *Travelling Light: Photography, Travel and Visual Culture*, (Manchester and New York: Manchester University Press, 2000).

37   Paine, Jeffrey, *Father India*, (New Delhi: Penguin Books, 1999).

38   Pinney, Christopher, *Camera Indica*, (London: Reaction Books, 1997).

39   Pratt, Mary Louise, *Imperial Eyes: Travel Writing and Transculturation*, (London: Routledge, 1992).

40   Primeau, Ronald, *Romance of the Road: The Literature of the American Highway*, (Ohio: Ohio State University Press, 1996).

41   Rose, Jacqueline, *Sexuality in the Field of Vision*, (London: Verso, 1994).

42   Said, Edward, *Orientalism: Western Conceptions of the Orient*, (London: Penguin, 1995).

43   Schama, Simon, *Landscape and Memory*, (New York: Alfred A Knopf, Inc, 1996).

44   Sen, Indrani, *Women and the Empire: Representations in the Writings of British India (1858-1900)*, (New Delhi: Orient Longman, 2002).

45   Sontag, Susan, "The Anthropologist as Hero," *Against Interpretation: Essay in Criticsm*, (New York: Dell Publications, 1996).

46   Stevenson, Robert Louis, *Inland Voyage*, (London : Macmillan, 1957).

47   Suleri, Sarah, *The Rhetoric of English India*, (Chicago: The University of Chicago Press, 1992).

48   Theroux, Paul, *The Great Railway Bazaar: By Train Through Asia*, (London: Penguin, 1966).

49   Tinling, Marion, ed, *With Women's Eyes: Visitors to the New World, 1775-1918*, (Hamden: CT Archon Books, 1993).

50   Trojanow, Ilija, "Imperial Politics in the Progressive Gaze," *The Hindu Literary Supplement*, 2nd December 2001.

51   Wesley, Marilyn, *Secret Journeys: The Trope of Women's Travel in American Literature*, (Albany, New York: The University of New York Press, 1998).

52   Yegenoglu, Meyda, *Colonial Fantasies: Towards a Feminist Reading of Orientalism*, (Cambridge University Press, 1998).

53   Young, Robert, *White Mythologies*, (London: Routledge, 1995).

ARTICLES AND JOURNALS

1   Bouma, Jana A, and Dora-Dhoore Ramirez. "Reflections and Border Crossings," *College Literature*, Winter 2001: 219-227.

2   Carroll, Mary, "Ladies of the Grand Tour: British Women in Pursuit of Enlightment and Adventure in Eighteenth Century Europe," *Book List*, November 2001: 53-56.

3   Chard, Chloe, "Moving Lives: Twentieth Century Women's Travel Writing," *Times Literary Supplement*, November 2001: 31-48.

4   Felber, Lynette, "Capturing the Shadows of Ghosts," *Film Quarterly*, Summer 2001: 27-37.

5   Greger, Cristoph, "Constructing the Aesthetic Gaze: 'Salome' and the Submissive Art of Spectatorship," *Literature and Psychology*, Fall 2001: 38-51.

6   Hassam, Andrew, "Narrative Occasions and the Quest for Self-Presence in the Travel Diary," *Ariel: A Review of International English Literature*, October 1990: 37-43.

7   Kroller, Eva-Mary, "Writes of Passage: Reading Travel Writing," *Journal of Historical Geography*, April 2001: 279-93.

BIOGRAPHICAL NOTES

Mohammed Zaheer Basha is a Lecturer in the English Studies Department of Gulbarga University, Gulbarga, India. Travel Writing and Critical Theory are areas of his special interest. He is currently working on his PhD on Katherine Mayo's works on India.

Narendra Luther is a former Chief Secretary of Andhra Pradesh, India. He is an acknowledged expert on the history and culture of Hyderabad. He has written extensively on this subject and is the author of thirteen books including *Hyderabad - Memoirs of a City*, a novel, *Beyond the Full Circle*, and a pictorial, *Rockitecture of Andhra Pradesh*. Two books, *The Nocturnal Court*, and *Prince of Photographers* are under print. He has won several awards for his work in Urdu. Some of his books and articles have been translated into a number of Indian and foreign languages. He has also produced many acclaimed documentaries including India's first full-length animation film on the love story of the founder of Hyderabad. His documentary has won two "Golden Aster" awards at the Japan

International Festival in 1999. He writes a regular column for leading national newspapers.

Pallavi Pandit Laisram taught Rhetoric and Composition and Business Communication at Pennsylvania State University between 1984 and 1990. Later she taught spoken and written English to native and non-native speakers of the language at Montgomery College, Maryland, USA. At present she is an editor at the ICFAI Center for Management Research (ICMR), the research wing of the Institute for Chartered Financial Analysts of India. At ICMR she reviews case studies and textbooks developed for national and international audiences. She is currently preparing an anthology on business communication.

Pramod K Nayar, a *Visiting Smuts Fellow* in Commonwealth Studies, University of Cambridge, 2000-2001, is a lecturer in the Department of English at the University of Hyderabad, India. He is currently working on a project on British Travel Writing and India, 1600-1800. He reviews for *Studies in Travel Writing, Jouvert, Culture Machine, E-Green, Philosophy in Review* and other international journals.

Sachidananda Mohanty is a Professor of English at the University of Hyderabad, India. He was a *British Council Scholar* in UK, 1990, *Fulbright Post-Doctoral Fellow* at Texas and Yale, 1990-91 and *Salzburg Fellow*, Austria, 1996. He received the *Katha Award* for outstanding translation in 1992 and 1994, the *Katha British Council Translation Prize*, 1994 and the University Grants Commission's *Career Award*, 1994-97. He was a *Senior Academic Fellow* at the *American Studies Research Centre (ASRC)*, Hyderabad, 1999, and *Fellow, Cambridge Seminar on the Contemporary British Writer*, 1999. He has nine books to his credit including an edited work on the Indo-US Cultural Exchange, 1950-97 for the *US Educational Foundation in India (USEFI)*. His essays and articles have appeared in some of the leading journals and forums in the country. He has a forthcoming book entitled *Lost Tradition: Early Women's Writing in Orissa, 1998-1950*.

Sindhu Menon received her PhD from the University of Hyderabad, India. A major section of her thesis deals with travel documents, especially with those produced by early British women travellers to India. Currently she is a lecturer in English at Bangalore University, India, and has been involved in research projects dealing with empire and travel writing.

Susan Bassnett is Pro-Vice-Chancellor at the University of Warwick and Professor in the Centre for Translation and Comparative Cultural Studies, which she founded in the 1980s. She is the author of over twenty books and her *Translation Studies*, (3rd ed. 2002) has become the most important textbook around the world in the expanding field of Translation Studies. Recent books include *Studying British Cultures: An Introduction* (1997), *Constructing Cultures* (1998) written with André Lefevere and *Postcolonial Translation* with Harish Trivedi (1999). She writes columns for several national newspapers and her collection of poems and translations, *Exchanging Lives*, came out in 2002.

V B Tharakeshwar is a lecturer in the Department of Translations, Kannada University, Hampi, India. He has worked on issues of colonialism and nationalism in the context of colonial Karnataka and Kannada literature. He is currently working on a project *Colonialism and Translation in Kannada* and is also coordinating a national level group project on *Rethinking the "Crisis" in English Studies*. He translates between Kannada and English and has published several articles on the above issues.

Tutun Mukherjee is a Professor of English at Osmania University, Hyderabad, India. Her areas of specialization include: Literary Criticism and Critical Theory, Translation Studies, Women's Writing, Drama and Film Studies. Her publications include twenty nine papers published in journals and anthologies including the following: *I A Richards and New Criticism*, (1990); *The Chicago Critics: An Evaluation*,

(1992); *Translator, Mindscape: Short Stories of Premendra Mitra*, (2000). She has a forthcoming book: *Girish Karnad's Plays: Performance and Critical Perspectives* and is currently preparing an anthology of plays written by women.

William Dalrymple wrote the highly acclaimed bestseller *In Xanadu* when he was twenty two, which won him the 1990 *Yorkshire Post Best First Work Award* and a *Scottish Arts Council Spring Book Award*. His second book, *City of Djinns*, won the 1994 *Thomas Cook Travel Book Award* and the *Sunday Times Young British Writer of the Year Award*. From *the Holy Mountain*, his acclaimed study of the demise of Christianity in its Middle Eastern homeland, was awarded the *Scottish Arts Council Autumn Book Award* for 1997. In 2002 he was awarded the *Mungo Park Medal* by the Royal Scottish Geographical Society for his "outstanding contribution to travel literature." He wrote and presented the television series *Stones of the Raj* and *Indian Journeys*, which won the *Grierson Award* for Best Documentary Series at BAFTA in 2002. His Radio 4 series on the history of British spirituality and mysticism, *The Long Search*, recently won the 2002 *Sandford St Martin Prize* for Religious Broadcasting. He now divides his time between London and Delhi.

ABOUT KATHA

Katha, a registered nonprofit organization set up in September 1989, works in the areas of education, publishing and community development and endeavours to spread the joy of reading, knowing and living amongst adults and children. Our main objective is **to enhance the pleasures of reading for children and adults,** for experienced readers as well as for those who are just beginning to read. Our attempt is also to stimulate an interest in lifelong learning that will help the child grow into a confident, self-reliant, responsible and responsive adult, as also to help break down gender, cultural and social stereotypes, encourage and foster excellence, applaud quality literature and translations in and between the various Indian languages and work towards community revitalization and economic resurgence. The two wings of Katha are **Katha Vilasam** and **Kalpavriksham.**

KATHA VILASAM, the Story Research and Resource Centre, was set up to foster and applaud quality Indian literature and take these to a wider audience through quality translations and related activities like **Katha Books, Academic Publishing,** the **Katha Awards** for fiction, translation and editing, **Kathakaar –** the Centre for Children's Literature, **Katha Barani –** the Translation Resource Centre, the **Katha Translation Exchange Programme, Translation Contests. Kanchi –** the Katha National Institute of Translation promotes translation through **Katha Academic Centres** in various Indian universities, **Faculty Enhancement Programmes** through Workshops, seminars and discussions, **Sishya –** Katha Clubs in colleges, **Storytellers Unlimited –** the art and craft of storytelling and **KathaRasa –** performances, art fusion and other events at the Katha Centre.

KALPAVRIKSHAM, the Centre for Sustainable Learning, was set up to foster quality education that is relevant and fun for children from nonliterate families, and to promote community revitalization and economic resurgence work. These goals crystallized in the development of the following areas of activities. **Katha Khazana** which includes **Katha Student Support Centre, Katha Public School, Katha School of Entrepreneurship, KITES –** the Katha Information Technology and eCommerce School, **Iccha Ghar – The Intel Computer Clubhouse @ Katha, Hamara Gaon** and **The Mandals –** Maa, Bapu, Balika, Balak and Danadini, **Shakti Khazana** was set up for skills upgradation and income generation activities comprising the Khazana Coop. **Kalpana Vilasam** is the cell for regular research and development of teaching/ learning materials, curricula, syllabi, content comprising **Teacher Training, TaQeEd – The Teachers Alliance for Quality eEducation. Tamasha's World!** comprises Tamasha! the Children's magazine, *Dhammakdhum! www.tamasha.org* and ANU – Animals, Nature and YOU!

www.ingramcontent.com/pod-product-compliance
Lightning Source LLC
Chambersburg PA
CBHW030927090426
42737CB00007B/347